Rae of Hope

STORIES FROM SURVIVORS

MARIANNE CURTIS

Other books by Marianne Curtis

Finding Gloria

Moondust and Madness: A Collection of Poetry

Finding Gloria Special Edition

Behind Whispering Pines

Brian's Last Ride

A Discreet Betrayal

***

What you are reading is the testimonials of real-life experiences of the individuals who have courageously relayed their stories. Some names and identifying details have been changed to protect the privacy of individuals or in accordance with legal cases that may still be pending before the Canadian courts. The author and Emerald Publishing shall have neither liability nor responsibility to any person or entity with respect to any loss or damage caused, or alleged to have been caused, directly or indirectly, by the information contained in this book. If you do not wish to be bound by the above, you may return this book to the publisher for a full refund.

***

FIRST PRINTING

***

Rae of Hope

Copyright © November 2014 Marianne Curtis

Published by Emerald Publications

ISBN: 1494869357

ISBN-13: 978-1494869359

DEDICATION

This book is dedicated to every single person in this world, who has been affected by bullying at any stage of their lives.

You are not victims, you are survivors!

In loving memory of those who have died as a result of bullying.

***

"Sometimes in tragedy, we find our life's purpose...
The eye sheds a tear to find its focus" ~ Robert Brault

CONTENTS

BULLYING STOPS HERE

ACKNOWLEDGMENTS

Rae of Hope: Stories from Survivors is a collection of stories written by real people, who have suffered at the hands of bullies. The authors have either been bullied, or been bullies. They are also mothers who've watched their children suffer at the hands of bullies.

I would like to extend a special heartfelt thank you to the many contributors who stood up and bravely told their story from Canada, US and the United Kingdom. Jaclyn, Jessica, Valerie, Robb, Lovern, Oscar, Lottie, Candace, Deonina, Pebbles Dunn, Rae, Tanya, Casia, Christopher, Candace, Evan, Jenna, Leah, Jade and Gina - thank you for entrusting me with your stories; I am really honoured.

I know it was not easy to share, but your stories will make a difference! We are all survivors!

INTRODUCTION

At the end of 2013, the province of Manitoba approved Bill 18 a controversial amendment to the Public Schools Act, despite the fact that over three hundred people spoke out demanding amendments. For months the issue of bullying, protecting children, protecting religious rights and freedoms and allegations of hidden agendas plagued local media and social media.

I deliberately remained mute on this issue. The advantage of working freelance is that while my editor may send me stories to cover, I also have a choice on which issues I really want to pursue, and which I want to sit back and watch. Bill 18 was one I choose to watch.

Not because I was scared, or it was too controversial, for once, I found myself unable to write about it without becoming biased. You see, I have my own story to tell; and boy did I ever. On September 10, 2013 I stood before the Committee and poured out my heart. I recalled how I was bullied while attending school in Steinbach. Bullying is not the right word – I was tormented.

I won't get into the horrific details, but as I gave my presentation, it hit me – if I'd grown up during the time of social media, I probably would not be sitting here today.

Standing before those Members of the Legislative Assembly, not as a reporter, but as a victim took a lot of courage. It was the first time that I verbally called out the school division for failing to see past the obvious. I was not a problem child – I was an abused, broken child; someone that should have been protected and helped. Instead, I was tossed aside, considered hopeless and life moved on for my classmates and educators alike. I was just a broken cog in the system.

It took decades of healing to get past what I suffered at the hands of my classmates. My home situation was less than stellar so my challenges were many.

I would like to say that things have changed in thirty years, but watching all the comments, discussions and debates taking place throughout the region, I find myself sorely disappointed. You would think society would be kinder, but it is not. There are still children killing themselves because they feel that's the only way out.

I for one am grateful that Bill 18 has passed. I believe that it will be revisited and amended as time goes on, but in the mean time, the groundwork has been laid to at least start protecting other kids like me.

Thank you to everyone who had the courage to share their stories; our voices have been heard.

RAE OF HOPE

Speaking as a parent, I would venture to say that the worst thing that could ever happen in my life is that I would have to bury one of my children. No matter what the reason or the cause the death, the passing of a young one in the bloom of their youth would be a difficult cross to bear.

Death is never easy to deal with, no matter how old we are and as parents, we try to shelter our children from the horrors of life, and console them in the event of the passing of a family member, friend or schoolmate.

Recently I found myself dealing with a situation that I did not think I would ever have to handle. An innocent looking blue piece of paper from my daughter's elementary school informed parents that a student had taken her own life.

She was only twelve! I took a look at my girls – all three of which were in that age group and my heart ached.

The number one question is always "why?" What could possibly make a child hurt so much that they would resort to something as final as death? I asked my daughter, who was a fellow classmate, if she was aware of anything unusual. I was quickly informed that this young lady was a recent transfer student. A ward of Child and Family Services, she was placed in a foster home in the community. She was one of a handful of Aboriginal students in a student population of two hundred. It made me angry to hear how this girl was bullied, for being Native, for being a foster child, for not being a Christian. Everything I heard made me furious. Many people failed this child - the school, the foster parents, the system - even her fellow classmates.

Unable to cope for one more excruciating moment, she left school at the end of the day, went back to her foster home and hung herself.

As a reporter, I hated making that phone call to the school to confirm the sparse details. Then, after speaking to the school principal, I tried to understand and respect the way they dealt with this situation, but it was difficult. The school division brought in grief counsellors to speak to students, and a small memorial service just for her classmates was held. Other than that, nothing was said or done.

End of story. The book was closed. Or was it?

What about the rest of us? How do we pick up the pieces after such a senseless tragedy? Are our children at risk and we do not see it? These are all valid questions, but where do we find the answers? It was obvious answers would not come from the school division or the school.

What made me furious about the situation was how quickly the school swept it under the carpet. Sure, they got counsellors for the students, and held a memorial service, but they did not want to talk about it. This was a teaching moment; a moment that teachers could have talked to students about bullying, mental illness and suicide. Instead, within days, the incident was forgotten, and everyone moved on as if nothing happened.

It is my opinion that our "sheltered" Christian community had been shattered by something that no one wanted to talk about. It was easier to condemn the suicide victim to an afterlife in hell than to discuss what drove the person to suicide in the first place. If we as adults find it difficult to discuss something so tragic, how can we expect our children to move ahead like nothing happened?

Suicide brings a gamut of emotions, and feelings to the surface. Most people do not even want to deal with it. It is almost like a failure, when someone you know has taken such a drastic step. Death is so final, and at one's own hands... it is almost unthinkable. There is nothing glamorous about suicide. My family has been touched by this before, and I will never forget the pain, hurt, and betrayal that was felt by all when dealing with this crisis.

But a carpet is no place to hide the truth. We do not live in a bubble and this is something that we all need to deal with. If we hide from the truth, it will reach out and bite us one day; and we will not know how to act.

One thing that I learned from this situation was to take my children more seriously. If they have a problem, it is my job as their parent to help them cope. To teach them the tools they need to survive in this world. It is our responsibility as parents, and as a community. It is our responsibility to make sure that our children feel loved, and protected so that they do not feel that they need to resort to the same method of action.

It may seem like the end of the world when a crisis too big for us to handle, comes along unexpectedly, but there are places you can call that will listen and help you deal with the issue at hand. Crisis lines are available for all ages, so please do not hesitate making the call for yourself or to help a friend.

Life is too short and precious – call someone who cares from the Kids Help Phone at **1-800-668-6868.**

MARIANNE CURTIS

MARIANNE

My name is Marianne Curtis; for the past 19 years I have been the head-writer for the *Dawson Trail Dispatch*, a monthly newspaper from the southern corner of Manitoba. I am also the author of several books, including my personal bestselling memoir, Finding Gloria.

When I sat down to write my life story in *Finding Gloria*, I did so with the purpose to find out why I was having issues with certain things in my life. Once I opened up my heart and allowed it to speak through my pen, I was finally able to come to grips with my past and it became a significant milestone in my personal healing process. With forgiveness, I found my freedom.

As a result, much to my surprise, I was even nominated for a *Woman of Distinction Award* in 2013 by people who read my story. This was an honour I felt I did not deserve and yet, it gives testament about how far I have come.

It was important for me to stand up and say - I was bullied! I was bullied to the extreme and no thanks to the public school system, I survived. This went on for six years – while I attended school at three different local community schools.

I was punched, hit, had my hair cut off, had my clothes torn or stolen; I was stripped naked by classmates and mocked for being bruised and skinny; I was bullied off a high diving board and almost drowned.

There were boys who got a sadistic pleasure out of punching me until I cried every single day. They'd steal my meagre lunch and stomp or spit on it; once it was swapped out with dog faeces. I was deliberately pushed down the stairs at school; I was locked in a closet so I'd miss the bus, I was even pushed into traffic. I had school projects, textbooks, homework and library books destroyed by classmates because they could get away with it. In grade 5, my teachers put me in the back of the class with a wall around my desk; they believed that by keeping me away from the class, students would be nicer. It made things worse.

I went to school daily in constant terror; I could not tell my teachers or principals because when I did, they either did not believe me or my parents were called in which made things worse. What no one knew at the time was that at home, things were even worse. My adoptive mother suffered from mental illness and while she did not drink or do drugs, she had a vicious temper and knew how to use a rubber hose or a leather strap. When I went home, I was beaten, starved, locked in the basement or out of the house; there was no escape from the emotional and physical abuse – at school or at home.

I was picked on because I was ugly, I was Ukrainian, I was adopted, I was Catholic, I wore dresses, I was stupid, I was not related to anyone in town, I did not go to any of the local churches, I wore glasses, we were farmers, I was poor; I did not have boobs, I did not have friends, the teachers hated me, the students hated me – I heard it all and every day was excruciating.

10

Did I mention that most of my tormentors came from God fearing Christian families?

In grade 10, I was raped in the second floor bathroom of my high school. I was suspended. When I came back to school, the bullying was even worse (yes, that was possible), now people threw money at me, called me horrible names, I became a moving target for every pubescent pervert in the school until finally, a grade 12 boy was caught in the act of sexually assaulting me. I was deemed the problem and immediately expelled while my attacker got to graduate.

This is how the school dealt with the problem. I was never offered help, counselling or even an opportunity to explain what happened. Unfortunately, once I was at home full time, the abuse at home worsened and eventually I was forced to run away – I was afraid my mother would kill me and no one would know or care. I ended up in foster care and for the first time in my life, people started to listen to me, and give me the help and protection that I needed.

This was thirty years ago.

Needless to say, when I heard the Province of Manitoba was planning on passing a controversial anti-bullying bylaw in Manitoba I was elated. FINALLY, someone was going to do something to protect kids like me; kids who have been beaten into mental submission to the point that it ruined their lives and stripped them of all hope.

It breaks my heart when I hear that kids are killing themselves because they are not being heard, or they are being bullied into it. Girls killing themselves because they've been taken advantage of or raped; social media bullying, kids who believe it is easier to die than tell their families they are gay. Kids should not feel that death is their only recourse when something horrific happens to them. They should be protected, not ostracized.

This is what I'd hoped Bill 18 would achieve. Unfortunately, what it has done is cause even more conflict. Over the past few months, I have been disgusted by the attitudes coming from various communities. Because of the simple inclusion of the Gay-Straight Alliance in the Bill, bigots' young and old have surfaced. To suggest as some have, that allowing the gay-straight alliance to have a group within the schools will lead to paedophilia and bestiality groups is ludicrous. While I understand the importance of stressing that the Gay-Straight alliance be included, excluding other groups of equal importance gives the appearance of pushing certain agendas, and not addressing bullying as a whole.

Addressing bullying is very important; protecting our children is even more important. If the school system is not prepared to handle certain situations, then someone else has to step in and do it for them, or set appropriate guidelines. Look at what happened to me – no one ever told me I could have pressed charges, no one offered me counselling, no one even wanted to talk about what happened. I was considered a threat to the student population, deemed promiscuous and tossed aside – no one EVER acknowledged that I was raped, until I published my book; then people started coming forward and apologized for not stepping forward and doing what was right at the time.

Unfortunately, the damage was already done. I had a reputation I did not earn, I had no self-esteem and to be frank, I saw no value in myself. Maybe if one teacher had said, "I believe you," or "Can we talk about what happened?" my life would have been very different. Maybe if there were protocols in place to deal with situations like this, I would not have lost about twenty years of my life and hated myself because the system failed to protect me.

At the same time, I am very grateful for that loss – it has given me the courage to find the healing I needed and the ability to find my voice. I sit here in spite of my bullies; I have proved to them, but mostly I have proved to myself that I am someone and that I matter.

They have not and will not win.

It is time for our communities and governments to step up to the plate and do something to protect kids like me; kids who have been beaten into mental submission to the point that it ruined their lives and stripped them of all hope.

Myth #1

"Children have got to learn to stand up for themselves."

Reality

Children who get up the courage to complain about being bullied are saying they've tried and can't cope with the situation on their own. Treat their complaints as a call for help. In addition to offering support, it can be helpful to provide children with problem solving and assertiveness training to assist them in dealing with difficult situations.

DEONINA

It's funny. I was bullied but in some way I never thought that it was bullying because it was so subtle. At least to a little girl. Being picked last in anything, being TOLD you're the "dad or male role" in anything.

Then there were the not so subtle ways. The name-calling, the throwing things, the stares, the comments, and everything else that could have gone on behind my back.

I kept being told that, "It would get better." "Wait a little longer," but if anything, it got worse and worse and worse. Until the day I found myself in the kitchen, surprising my parents with dinner, holding a paring knife, and that's when it hit me; it won't ever get better, I couldn't wait any longer, who cared about me? Who would miss me if I ended it all? It had to end. Then I got a text from someone who I cared about, who asked me if I was truly okay.

I soon asked myself, was I honestly at rock bottom with no further place to go down? Then I got to thinking. What would happen if I stuck it out just a little bit longer. What if I stuck around for one more day.

I'm glad I did.

For two days later, I found out about my long lost sister. There was hope. I found out that somebody had the bullying way worse than I did, to a further extreme than I did, and she survived. The road was long and hard, but she travelled on. She made it. Through the bullying and everything else... she became a survivor. And because of her I decided that if she could do it, then I could rise above everything that happened in the past and that was happening to me at the time, and actually LIVE my life... and not just cruise through it with no emotion.

So I stood up, made sure that no one was going to tear me down, and that I wouldn't let the little jabs and the little things bother me anymore.

But most importantly, I finally understood that it was up to me to decide whether the bullies won or not.

Guess what?

They didn't. And I'm glad! I think of what I would have missed out on if I had listened to them about my worth and whatever else they told me. I'd have missed out on college, high school graduation, meeting my sister and her family, and one day having my own. I wouldn't know the strength, love and the happiness I have now.

I won! I beat them.

I survived.

VALERIE

In senior high the teachers were in on a lot of the bullying I experienced - the teachers called them "pranks". The boys would hold me down and take measurements so they could weld me a bra. The teacher stood and watched and laughed while the boys tormented me. He never lifted a finger while they all took turns feeling or rubbing by breasts while I fought to get up. The ruckus attracted the attention of more fellow students in the classroom, but no one stood up for me.

I ended up getting kicked out of school for two days because I fought back and kicked two boys during the incident. I was forced to talk to the school counsellor to see how we could "fix" the problems. Instead of fixing the problems, I was blamed for them. I was told that I needed to be quiet and not instigate the torment. In other words, if someone hit or kicked me, I was the one sent to the office. Then I was told by the counsellor that kids would not bother me unless I had given them a reason. I must have done something to make them want to hurt me.

I was even called a "stupid retard" by my teachers!

All the years of abuse had caused me to have learning problems. Finding it difficult to learn in the hostile environment, I had to be shown

17

how to do things over and over. Instead of helping, I was told that I was a half-wit who did not belong in class - not just from my fellow classmates, but by my teachers.

I would skip school to get away from it, but there was no place to turn. When I was in grade 11, I tried taking my life.

I begged the counsellor at school to help me get away from school and home but no one listened. No one listened to me or believed me when I would tell them what was happening to me, so I became a bully to other bullies. I started hitting, kicking and yelling at people when they were bullying others. I did not see it as bullying. I believed I was protecting those being bullied yet the truth was, I was beating up the bullies.

Eight weeks before the end of grade 11, I was expelled from school. The day before I was kicked out of school, I was held down by five guys in the hallway of the high school. They hit and punched me. They slapped and groped me between my thighs and hurt my breasts. Instead of disciplining those who assaulted me, I was expelled. I was told I was being kicked out of school for my own protection.

I still wanted to graduate, but the only way I could come back to graduate was if I could prove I had changed. Admittedly, it was hard. My parents separated when I started grade 10, so I was angry at the world and no one would talk to me. When I was allowed back, I eventually graduated. I worked hard, kept to myself, went to all my classes, but I only spoke when spoken to. I did not want anything or anyone to keep me from my goal - getting my diploma and proving to everyone, especially myself that I was not the half-wit my teachers and classmates pegged me.

A few years later, when I had my first child, I was very protective of her; my second child as well. My children were teased a lot in school for having come from a single parent family. I lived with a bully and he abused me. I finally left him, once he tried to hit my oldest daughter.

I had no one to turn to. I was still leery about Child and Family Services (CFS) because they did not help me while I was growing up. Sure enough, neither CFS or the school stepped up to help when my daughters were both chased home from school by kids armed with a bat from school or chased with an axe. Even the local RCMP refused to help; saying it was nothing more than children playing.

What upsets me the most was that the school did not know how to handle bullying. Once again, instead of dealing with the bullies, they sent the victim home "to protect" them.

At twenty-six, I suffered a complete mental breakdown. I tried cutting my wrists to end up in the hospital in an effort to escape the bullying. Even then, no one wanted to help me. I was in hospital for two weeks while my kids stayed with family.

I have since forgiven the abuse and bullying. It has taken me many years of counselling to get over the bullying and abuse I suffered as a teenager and young adult. I can finally sleep in a room with the lights off and can even close the bedroom door. I am no longer worried about being unable to get away in a hurry and I am no longer afraid that I will have to get away from the boys.

Myth #2

"Children should hit back - only harder."

Reality

This could cause serious harm. People who bully are often bigger and more powerful than their victims. This also gives children the idea that violence is a legitimate way to solve problems. Children learn how to bully by watching adults use their power for aggression. Adults have the opportunity to set a good example by teaching children how to solve problems by using their power in appropriate ways.

JESSICA

Words hurt, actions hurt. It doesn't matter which of the two it ends up being. They stick with you for life!

One of the reasons that I was bullied was because as a child and young teenager, I had many phobias. I was scared of masks, wigs, clowns and costumes. Nobody understood it and to be honest, I didn't either. All I knew was that the fear was there.

A couple of incidents come to mind as I think back. It was in kindergarten and one of my friends was having a birthday party at her house. Little did I know that once I opened the front door that I would be greeted by her father, who was dressed up as a clown! He then held up his foot and said, "Shake my foot!" I stood there in complete horror. I remember standing in the corner of the basement behind a chair, while he sat on a couch nearby and tried to show me there was nothing to be scared of. Eventually he went upstairs to change. I know that this doesn't have much to do with bullying but it's one of the first instances that I can think of.

One of the first instances that comes to mind with bullying that ties into this, was in grade 4. I was sitting at my desk, like everyone else, minding my own business. I was shy. There was a group of girls, who were a year older than me, standing there giggling. Then I saw them with one of the girls' wigs. I guess they saw my look of terror and thought it was funny. They began tossing it back and forth to each other in front of me, whenever the teacher turned his head. Once the teacher was done the lesson and sat at his desk, I got the nerve to get up and go tell him what was going on. This was the first time in school that I had gone to the teacher and was brave enough to say something.

They then called the girl, the owner of the wig, into the hallway. I could see them both through the window and each had a smile on their face and were laughing. Then they came back into the classroom and the girl looked at me with a smirk on her face. I knew in that moment that everything had changed and that school life was not going to be easy.

Another instance, was also in that same class. It was around Christmas time and the teacher was lining everyone up to go to the Christmas concert rehearsal in the gymnasium. I peered at the window into the hallway and noticed some of the kids were dressed as clowns. I started panicking. I couldn't get into the line up. The line up led to them - my fear. I tried to get the teacher's attention. Once I did, I tried to pull him aside so that none of the other kids would hear me. As I told him what was going on - he told me in a stern voice, "Jessica! Stop your crying and get into the line-up!" He never took the time to understand what a phobia truly is and never took the time to understand me or how I felt.

There were many more instance's throughout my childhood. Chased by other kids in the schoolyard wearing masks. I was laughed at and excluded. Even parents would turn to look at me to see my reaction. I was picked last for most things. I was different and everyone seemed to know it.

Halloween consisted of going to McDonald's and bowling with my family and quickly shutting off all the lights in our home while I sat there in complete terror. One Halloween, at McDonald's, I saw a group of teenagers walk in all dressed up - one was Ronald McDonald. I ran outside, shaking. My ice-cream sundae running down the front of my jacket. My dad came running out to make sure I was alright. Fear is not fun to live with.

After going to see a couple of school counsellors - one even suggested bringing all of my phobia's into the room to see if it would help and she asked me how it made me feel. In Grade 7, my parents decided to take me to a counsellor at the Health Sciences Centre. I would leave school early every Tuesday to go talk to him to try and figure out where it all started and to understand who I was as an individual.

In the end, I wanted to try to get over it on my own. I went home one day and told my Mom to stand at the end of the hallway, holding an alien mask that my sister had stored away. I took small steps towards it until I finally was standing right in front of it. Next I thought, "This is it! The end of all my fears, the end of being laughed at." I reached out my hand and I touched it!

Later in that same year, I had a role in a school project where in the end of the film, I wore the mask of the killer. This I find very fitting, I did "kill" something - the fear that had so much power over me and my life for so many years.

Ironically enough, one of those kids who had chased me around the schoolyard wearing a mask turns out to be my best friend. She feels awful about what she did so many years ago.

Bullying isn't worth it.

Hurtful words said, or cruel actions done will stick to you or someone else for the rest of your life, whether you're the bully or the victim. Neither party feels good about it, and will even regret that it ever happened. Think about what you do or say before you do it. Just ask yourself first, "Is this something that I want? To hurt someone with that will stick with them for the rest of their life?" or "Do I want to wake up full of regret?" Question how your cruel words or actions have had a negative impact in someone else's life. Think before you do.

Create happy memories and think of each person as an individual. If you think about your hardships in life, you realize everyone has them. If someone looks left out or alone - make the effort to go and talk to them. You might make their day or even save their life. You never know - they might turn into your best friend of the day. They're just misunderstood.

Don't be a follower - be a leader.

ROBB

L ooking at me today, with my appearance and attitude, one would automatically assume I was never bullied in grade school and high school. Yet the truth is, I was. I was a sickly kid in my early teens on up until mid teens. The doctors took nearly three years to figure out I was hypoglycaemic which caused fainting, odd outbursts and mood swings. Once I was diagnosed I gained almost 40lbs, being 5'7" and 160 lbs. This was difficult, because in school looking normal and athletic is important. It also matters to the girls. I grew up a loner being teased by the guys, while the girls taunted me by saying I would never have a girlfriend. Thus, started the mental cruelty that followed me for a few years.

Having hardly any friends and being taunted and teased, I learned to find things to do by myself. I liked to read and ride my bike and those things you can do alone. In grade 10 the physical abuse started joining the mental abuse. Being told that you're ugly and stupid every day has an effect on a young psyche. To this day I doubt myself and don't think I am a good-looking guy. Every day I was checked into lockers and punched (aka the charley horse or sissy test). I would go home and immerse myself in my own world in my room alone, away from all the jerks at school. Even the teachers were judgmental and made snarky remarks, along with one of the secretaries who said I would never amount to anything. After I left that town, I have rarely gone back to this day. I also never had to move back in with Mommy and Daddy because I could not cut it in the real world.

The saving grace for me was that both sets of grandfathers as well as an uncle and my father were all pretty tough in their youth and all with military connections. I can remember my grandfather telling me to be myself and if someone didn't like me, to hell with them. If they made fun of me, respond back with my sharp tongue and quick wit. If they wanted to make it physical, fight back. You may get beat, but they will learn that you will no longer be an easy target. I got beat somewhat early on but over time I learned that I could take a punch and throw one back. I learned that people that wanted to tease could not stand when it was done back.

After a while people stopped picking on me, but coming from a small town, if you're not part of a clique well then you are nothing. I didn't care. I just put up a wall and let people think I was angry and mean all the time and soon people started to stay away... rumours can be used to your advantage. To this day, people are not willing to tangle with me or bother my family. I put up a wall and it served me well.

Since moving to the city, I have made new friends, but because of the bullying, it takes a long time for me to trust people. I have a handful of true friends and a lot of acquaintances. I'm in a better place, but the recent media attention to the anti-bullying campaign to tell a teacher, etc. I feel is crap. It doesn't work. The fact is, if you tattle, you get it worse. The solution is to fight back, nobody wants to pick on someone who will fight back. Trust me. I am living proof.

I can look back now and blame how I turned out, directly on the way I was treated - I am a recovering alcoholic.

To this day I don't exactly know how to act in a social setting in large groups. I don't think of myself as better than the bullies, who by the way are still in that small area called Red Lake. Incidentally, the girls who thought they were too good and so "hot" back in high school, well, let's just say many need to look in the mirror, then attend weight watchers. Maybe this seems mean, but I speak my mind.

For the kids and adults that are bullied, I offer this... you deserve respect and the only way to get it is to earn it. I wish you the best.

Myth #3
"It builds character."

Reality
Children who are bullied repeatedly, have low self-esteem and do not trust others. Bullying damages a person's self-concept.

JACLYN

When I was told the name of this book, I KNEW it was something I had to contribute to. You see, my name is Jaclyn Rae, and I know what Hell is.

I was born to a mother who wasn't supposed to have kids, and a father who was a decade older than her, and had decided he needed to settle down and reproduce. Sounds ideal, right? Wrong. They were married November of 1985 and I was born in November of 1986. From the time they were married, they fought. A lot. And not just verbally, but physically too.

By the time my sister was born in May of 1988, they'd proven to be the perfect example of the term "toxic relationship" and had both started taking it out on me too. My baby sister and I became inseparable, because it was the only time we weren't getting spanked, made to kneel on a heat register, slapped, screamed at, or being hit with wooden spoons, brooms, pitchforks or whatever was within reach.

By three, I remember being nose first into the corner while the news started, ended, was replaced by another show and was finished before I was let out. It'd started with something I don't remember, but by the end, both my mom and dad were screaming at me, and each other. Somehow, even

29

with a toddler's mind, I mustered my courage, and standing there in my red and white footsie pyjamas, I looked at my parents and said, "If you hate me so much, go get your gun and shoot me. Then I'll be dead like Bambi's Mommy."

My mother then physically kept my father from going to their room where the gun cabinet was. As I got older, it only escalated. I've been told a lot as I've gotten older that my sister and I were always sleeping when anyone came to visit. So I don't have many memories of socializing with anyone other than my sister until I hit kindergarten. I fell into the tail end of the bracket having a birthday in November, and started kindergarten at 4. I knew no one, and had no idea how to interact with anyone and no one talked to me. I had hair down to my bum, third-hand clothes that hadn't been cool in over a decade, liked trucks and dinosaurs, and no one talked to me. At all.

My one upside to kindergarten was that my teacher was engaged to one of my cousins, so I got the special privilege of hiding in the downstairs of the playhouse instead of having to sit with the kids who made fun of me and threw matchbox cars at me during playtime when the teacher wasn't looking. I was the social outcast, before I even knew the words.

Grades one to four, I was ignored by everyone, and when I wasn't, I was pushed, tripped, poked, had people sit behind me and play with their scissors at their desks, and plug their noses, saying things like, "Ewwwww she smells like a farm!" Even though I'd had a bath right before bed.

With one exception, that being the birth of my brother in 1993, it only got worse, and one day, when there wasn't a stall for me to change in; I had to change for gym in the open. My back, butt and legs were all bruised from a spanking (it broke a wooden spoon) and the swings from a pitchfork handle, that I'd endured within that week. Several years later, during X-rays,

I'd learn that both my shins were fractured that week, from the force of the blows from that handle. They immediately reported it to a teacher, and suddenly everyone was my "friend".

Child and Family Services interviewed me at school, and interviewed my parents, who declared I was a pathological liar and made me write and read an apology to my classmates. They made me say that the bruises were from playing at home. Now I was a freak AND a liar.

The bullying got worse and even the other outcasts started to join in, and by grade 6, I was so desperate to escape that I stole all the leather and canvas belts out of the house (except my dad's), linked them together and had them hanging out of a tree in the far back pasture with a rotted stump rolled under it, and pencilled in a date - June 20. I figured it was close enough to the end of the year that no one would notice if I missed a day or two of school. I'd already picked a tree far enough from the road or the edge of the stand of trees for anyone to notice me right away. Somehow, my mother found out, and in a moment void of paranoia, anger, or violence, she made me swear I would not kill myself. I think she was worried what the community would think, and what an investigation would turn up if I did.

In grade 7, a new girl started in my grade, and the dynamics changed slightly. I developed a friendship with her, along with a girl who'd been held back a year. By midway through grade 8, one had moved away; and the other was my "best friend" and her visits to the farm were our reprieve from the beatings. At the end of grade 8, I switched schools, and started enduring vicious rumours, having gum thrown in my hair, and my legs stomped on as I sat with my back against my locker and my nose in a book, which by that time was my sole escape, and one more thing I was tormented for. I made one friend at that school, and to this day she is like family, and her children call me "auntie".

We finally convinced my mother that we had to leave, or someone would end up dead after some particularly vicious beatings, and when I informed my "best friend" that we would be leaving, she promptly ended our friendship, saying that divorce was bad, and shouldn't ever be allowed. We left on my fifteenth birthday, and I started school on the first day of the second semester of grade 10. I met some of the most important people ever, who took me under their wings. They also accepted the fact that I was raising my siblings - my mother quit being a mom when we left the farm - and that my whole home life was dysfunctional. They're still by my side now, as my family continues to war amongst themselves. My mother has decided to disown her children as I continue to slowly heal and rebuild a semblance of a relationship with my dad, and his family.

I will never doubt that the nine years without contact with my father was a good thing. The time apart was needed so I could try and heal, but I recognize that I am still far from completing the long long journey needed for healing. I now have amazing friends, and "family" to complement the genetic lines I have. However, I still have days where I curl up and cry for the sad scared and lonely little girl hiding deep inside of me.

But it gets better as I get older, and one day, I hope I'll be able to think back without crying.

OSCAR

Hi there, my name is Oscar; and I am a thirteen-year-old boy in seventh grade. My life was a living hell for about six years and it all started when I got to Milwaukee, Wisconsin.

It was the first day of school and I was excited to go to my new school, so I woke up and went to the bathroom to get ready for school. After I got ready, my grandma took me to school. Everything seemed to be fine the first few days of school, but the next week was when my living hell started.

All of the advance readers had to be sent to a higher grade for reading period, so my friend Alejandro and I went to third grade. At first, everything seemed to be ok, but then the kids started to tell me that I was an "ugly homosexual bitch". At first I thought they were just kidding, but then they started to say nastier things. They would call me fag, gay, girly girl and a whole bunch more. They weren't the only ones though. My classmates thought it was funny to call me bitch, motherfucker, and whore.

It was really sad to think that people at that young age could be so cruel and call you all those mean things. I never told anyone because I thought they weren't going to understand. So the years flew by and each

33

day, my life would become worse and worse.

Sometimes, I would cry all night long, or go running to the bathroom and lock myself in there. Other times I would fake I had stomach aches to get out of school early. It was really hard for me to live like this.

There were even times when I had suicidal thoughts. I would just want to disappear from this cruel world so I could live in peace. Over the years things got better, but it was still too much for me!

So I decided to cut myself. I only did it for a month thanks to my friends because if it hadn't been for them I would of probably killed myself a long time ago.

Today I realize I have the greatest friends who care about me. Thanks to them I am who I am today!

LOTTIE

One of my earliest memories is walking off the school bus; it must have been either year one or two, and getting punched in the stomach by a girl in year five or six. I can still remember that to this day, she didn't get reprimanded. My parents said that once, I came home soaking wet as the other students on the bus decided it would be fun to throw their water bottles over me; again none of them got told off. I remember sitting in the nursery on my own because I didn't have any friends who wanted to be around me.

All through my life I have been called names, fat, slag, spaz, retard, pig. When I was at my first school I got told nobody cared about me, not even my own parents. I got told I was useless, worthless and that if I left they would all have a party because they would be so happy I was gone. I had my possessions taken from me and thrown away.

All the time the school didn't believe me, they said I was lying. I became defensive, if someone bullied me, I would lash out at them. I got into so much trouble, I remember sitting outside the head teacher's office most lunchtimes writing lines. I remember being told I was a naughty child, that I was no smarter than any other kid in the school.

My best memory of this school was getting two desserts one day because I was writing lines outside the canteen and they had leftovers. I don't remember playing with the other children. I don't remember being invited by the other children to birthday parties, or play dates. I was a loner, with everyone, even the school, bullying me.

The school was blackmailing my parents and they finally had enough of it so they moved me. I started a new school where I didn't know anyone. My first term was okay, then it started again, they called me names, I got followed around the playground. I thought I had a friend though, but I was wrong. She went to the headmaster and told him I was bullying her. I got told to stay away from her; and I lost the one friend I had. Again, I had nobody.

A little way into this school I also got diagnosed as having Asperger's Syndrome, a high functioning form of autism. The school tried to create a friendship circle for me; however, this didn't last long when the people in there started bullying me. They called me names and again, I lashed out, I got excluded and they got nothing. The only breaks I remember at that school were sitting with a teacher as I was constantly in trouble for standing up to the bullies.

I moved schools again in year 6 to a private school, which had both primary and secondary schools. They said they could support my needs and that I should start a year early to get used to the school. They couldn't support me, they failed me. It was an all girls' school so it was very much verbal bullying. I got called names, got told that I wasn't as good as them as I didn't have as much money, I didn't have all the nice stuff they had. But finally I had friends, I found people who accepted me for who I was, people who were real friends that have still not left me. They stood up for me; they invited me to hang out with them.

However, I still had too many problems; the final straw at that school was when we had a swimming gala. We were watching the lower years and one of the girls left her seat and went to sit with her friends. I went and sat in her seat as she had been gone for so long, she came back and said to me, "That's my seat get out." I told her she had gone and sat with other people so it's not her seat anymore. She grabbed the back of the seat and tipped it up, throwing me out of the chair. I started shouting at her and I got taken out. They made me apologise to her, then the deputy head came back the next week and told me I had to apologise again. I went up to her and apologised but she refused to accept my apology and I stormed off pushing past her. I was then told I could not go back unless I had full time one to one support, which we would have to pay for. We couldn't afford that. I left there a few weeks early missing the musical I was a part of and which I had been looking forward to.

It was too late in the year to search for a new school by then so my parents home schooled me for the first term of year 7 whilst we looked for a school. However, there were no places at the schools around me so I ended up at the school I was in the catchment for. This was the school all the people who had bullied me at my first school had gone too. I was scared everything would be like my first school. I went there in defensive mode, I didn't trust anyone. Whenever someone tried to get close to me, I found a reason they shouldn't. People made fun of me, I can't remember much as it's all a blur, I put it to the back of my mind trying to forget everything that went on. I remember getting into lots of fights, people getting told that if they ask me out they would get money, like it was a game for them to play with my feelings. People treated me like I was nothing, like I didn't have feelings and I was just there for them to have some fun. I became more and more frustrated, I lashed out more. The school couldn't handle me; they couldn't handle what the bullies had turned me into. They had taken the happy little girl and made her into a monster, I am still that monster sometimes today, but I am working hard to try and be that happy little girl again. I want her back.

The Local Education Authority (LEA) moved me to a school with a special ASD unit, which is designed for children with autism. Everyone knew I was in there, everyone knew I was different. When I arrived there I didn't trust anyone, I couldn't trust anyone. I thought I had a friend, I thought she was a good friend but in fact she was slowly making me dislike her. Angry and resentful. I told her I no longer wanted to be her friend at the end of that year, she said to me she had never been my friend in the first place and that she was made to be my friend. Any trust I may have been gaining I lost in that instant.

Because they knew I was different they saw this as a weakness, as something to pick on. I was still in defensive mode and so when someone picked on me, I lashed out. I hit them, punched them, shouted and screamed. Anything to show them I wasn't weak, I was strong. But inside I was still a scared little girl who wanted to be loved and accepted. I got physically bullied here; there were times that I went home early because I was so traumatised I couldn't stay in school any longer. I got punched in the eye and had to go to the doctor, I refused to go into school the next day, I was terrified. I have been hit over the head many times, kicked in the stomach, hit, punched etc.

Then in year 10, we were in the changing rooms and I had an argument with one of the girls as she was picking on me because of my Aspergers, she came towards me and punched me. By this time I had learned not to hit back as I would get told off, I curled up on the floor in a ball to try and protect myself. She put her knee on my back to hold me down and was hitting me round the head. There were at least 10 other people in the changing room at that time. They stood and watched. They could have done something, they could have helped, but they didn't. She only stopped when the teacher came into the room.

I was beaten up so badly I had to go to the hospital twice. My mum took me the hospital the first time as my neck was stiff, then I went the second time as I was having difficulties breathing. I found out that she had cracked my ribs. I still have flashbacks of the incident even now; I remember how much it hurt me and I blame myself for what I said and for not stopping her. Until she left I was scared to walk around corners in case she was there waiting. Even after she left it still haunts me. The younger ones used it against me to pick on me; I can't get away from it.

She got one day in inclusion. I've been left scarred for life, terrified that she will find me when I'm out and beat me up again.

Even some of the teachers bullied me. I was at the reptile club one lunchtime and I was cleaning my hands when the TA told me to hurry up. I told her don't worry, I don't have a lesson next I'm just cleaning my hands. She said I will have a word with you back at the ASD unit. When we got back up there she told me that I shouldn't shout across the classroom, I told her that the sink was on the other side of the classroom so I had no choice. She told me not to backchat. I said fine then next time I won't wash my hands and if I die it's on your head. She told me that at least it would be quieter if I died. I ran off and the head of the ASD unit found me and told me I had overreacted and that it was only a joke. Why would you joke that you would prefer if someone was dead? This TA has also called me names like a nasty piece of work and questioned all my life's dreams. She would constantly belittle me and make me feel worthless and like I wouldn't achieve anything.

Then I started sixth form. I thought it would all go away as I would be older and the people I'm with would be more mature. How wrong was I? After the first couple of weeks I hated sixth form. I got called a train conductor because I wore a suit; people were still sniggering at me behind my back. Nothing had changed. While waiting for the bus and on the bus I would have water and biscuits thrown at me, they even threatened to throw a shoe at me once. I constantly feel left out like I don't belong, like I'm not from here. It got so bad I would just stay in the common room and put my headphones on to get away from the world.

Things started to change in March. After an awful lunchtime of getting called a lesbian for cutting my hair and called other names because of my suit, I was wandering the halls as I was too upset to sit in one place. One of the boys in sixth form saw me and asked if I was okay, everyone asks me this so it didn't seem like anything unusual. I told him yes, like I say to anyone as I don't want to bother them with my troubles. Then he got me to promise I was okay, nobody had ever done that before. I just said yes, as at that time I didn't want to have to explain anything. Then later on he saw me again and he asked if I wanted to go up to sixth form with him and his best friend. We went up there and he had people he needed to talk to but his friend made a seesaw from one of the seats and I played on that with him for the last five minutes of the day.

I messaged them on Facebook after the day and he told me it's not a problem and to let him know if I ever want to talk. I was saying about how it's just nice when someone shows me they care. I have a subconscious thought that nobody cares due to what happened in my life. My trust issues come from people not caring about me. This guy had shown and told me that he cares. In a matter of days I started to actually believe that someone does care about me, and that if one person cares about me others must do too. I started talking to him about my problems and he has got me help, I now have people who understand what I'm going through.

I feel as though I'm worth it, the voices that once told me I was useless are getting drowned out by the positive thoughts of someone cares enough to help, I must be worth something to someone. I will get through this; I will be that happy little girl again.

***

This story was submitted from the United Kingdom so some of the terminology may be different than readers are used.

Myth #4

"Sticks and stones can break your bones but words can never hurt you."

Reality

Scars left by name-calling can last a lifetime.

DEBRA

Bullying in the name of God?

Since moving out to a community that is high in religious beliefs. I, more than ever, have concluded how much I detest religion. Both my children have been given a lesson first hand about the effects of being bullied - in the name of God.

When we first came to this community, we arrived with great ideas and wanted to embrace the country life. Turns out, if there was a hell on earth, my youngest daughter is visiting it every day in elementary school.

I myself have been told by people in this community that I am going to hell and so will my children. Why? Because I was asked what I believe. I didn't think it was any stranger's business to ask me that, in fact, I only purchased a couple of chickens from the lady. I was caught off guard. I didn't know how to answer the question and felt a bit uneasy. I ended up answering her. I said I was spiritual. I already knew most people were religious in my area. How would they react to someone with an opposite view? Why should l even feel that I cannot be myself? After all, I am 40; am I not entitled to believe what I want?

So when I spewed out my answer in nervousness that is when I was told that I was the worst kind. I would go to hell and so would my children. I then got into my mustang as quickly as I could, fearing for myself and drove home with my chickens thinking, I am glad these chickens are no longer with the crazy lady. I didn't sleep well for two weeks after that. I had a very bad taste in my mouth.

I was at the local Co-op a few months back. A young single mother was crying at the post office while purchasing stamps. She was sobbing because of the things she was being told by some of the locals. She was not accepted here by some, as she was simply a single mother. Well, so am I. So what! Whose business is that?

A single mother is that of a person who is much stronger than most ever will be.

From the beginning, my youngest child had it the worst. Since day one in school. Her first few days of school consisted of torment that she would go to hell. Torment that has continued for two years now. The funny thing is, my youngest never once told me she didn't believe in God before moving here. She came to her own conclusion, from what the "believers" have shown.

My youngest is supposed to be attending a public school and I question that. Does a public school play Christian music in the class? My daughter gets reprimanded because she speaks out about it. A teacher once pulled her into the hallway and said she should believe in God. They badger her about it. This so-called public school also has a religious program every Wednesday evening inside the school. Should that not be held at the local community building?

My youngest has been stolen from, hit, pushed, kicked, emotionally abused, slapped, teased and so on. One Friday, she was pinned down in the schoolyard ground, with the hands of a so-called godly girl clamped over her face and mouth. Kids were laughing at her, standing there and watching but not doing anything. My daughter is the only non-religious girl in her class and the kids all know it and abuse her for it. One girl says to her, "We laugh at you, not with you." They also say, "My mother bans me from being your friend."

Now, I cannot say that there has been no retaliation on my daughter's side. However, a kid can only take so much bullying before she loses her temper. When she does, she is the one who gets expelled for the day.

I have tried to deal with these issues with my children's school. Nothing changes. They don't appear to care. Staff is mainly religious. When they do appear to care at the moment, it is fleeting in my eyes. When my children don't show up for school, the school never even calls to see where they are. I feel it is not safe to send her back to school on Monday until something drastic changes...but how and what?

Is this how God believes adults and children act? Sure, children will be children but where are these children learning to behave this way? To pick on you because you don't believe there is a God? They learn it from their parents.

I always believed that "God believing" people are supposedly kind, and open their hearts to others no matter what, without judgement. I have been shown, that I was wrong. My children have also been shown that as well.....the truth. The real truth.

Religion is destructive.

Myth #5

"That's not bullying. They're just teasing."

Reality

Vicious taunting hurts and should be stopped.

RAE

Bullying can be destructive and harmful to a person's life. It can get to the point where we, as human beings don't feel wanted, loved, or needed. We sometimes take words too seriously and often let what people say to us damage how we see ourselves. Sometimes people take what other people said to them or about them to their graves. My name is Rae and this is my story.

When I was around six months old my sister and I were adopted. I am the youngest of four sisters and one brother. I didn't really have any knowledge of being adopted until I was around thirteen years old. When I found out I didn't really think anything of it because the family I was adopted into is the only family I really knew. My parents had told my sister and I how our mom was addicted to drugs and how she wanted a better life for us so she gave us to people who could raise us in a good environment. I also found out my biological mother died from a drug overdose not too long after we were adopted. I'm glad to have been adopted into such a great family because without them who knows where I'd be today.

My life was great when I was a kid. Life took a huge turn when I was eleven years old. In the middle of my sixth grade year was when the bullying began. People I thought were my friends would write me mean notes and tell me I was fat or that I wasn't good enough. A rumour started spreading because I had had my first kiss in sixth grade. I would get guys asking me to do stuff with them or called a slut or a whore. At first I tried really hard to ignore the words, but after two years of continuous words I no longer could deal with the notes or words people would say to me.

Two years later the bullying still didn't go away. At this point I was having people message me on Facebook and calling me on my cell phone and leaving me with threats. They would call me late at night and tell me to watch my back and that they were going to send people to beat me up or that I'm not even going to be safe in my own home. This was when I started self harming to deal with the things they would say, I was thirteen. I started cutting or burning myself. Two of my friends found out I was harming myself and they decided they couldn't be friends with me anymore.

After that I really tried to stop harming myself and for a while I tried to be happy. But the words came back to haunt me. I had girls I didn't even know telling me I was fat, or calling me a freak and stupid. People would tell me that they're only saying that because they're jealous, but that's not what I wanted to hear. I wanted to hear a real reason for why they said the things they said to me so for a while I pinned what they said on myself.

By ninth grade I started skipping meals because I thought I was fat. I was cutting more and I never really felt safe going to school. I didn't know who to talk to about it. I went to my school counsellor about the bullying and all he said was they're only words, get over it. After that I just decided to keep to myself. I used to think maybe if I hadn't been adopted how different things would have been, if it maybe would have been better.

Once I got to my sophomore year I was having thoughts of suicide and my anxiety was getting really hard to deal with. I was constantly thinking the world would be better off without me and I was always worrying about not being good enough. My self-esteem began to lower and whenever I would look in the mirror, I would want to break down and cry.

I remember telling one of my best friends that I thought the world would be a much better place without me in it. She got really scared and told her mom about it. Her mom ended up calling the counsellor at school. He called me in his office, but I was too scared to talk, I just told him everything was fine. I ended up telling my mom about feeling depressed and anxious all the time, so she went and put me in counselling, I went for a while but I didn't feel like it was working. A few months after I started purging and I didn't feel like I could stop harming myself.

My junior year of high school, I was dating this guy. I was happy and I really tried to stop cutting. I continued to go to counselling to try to work on myself. Then things took a huge turn. After three or four months of dating he sexually assaulted me, twice. The first time it happened, he apologized and sounded sincere, so I decided to let it go. Big mistake. The second time it happened we were at a lake fishing, it was six days after my seventeenth birthday. The night I got home, I went straight to my room. I told three people that night, but I told them not to tell anyone. My biological sister knew something was up so she came in my room to talk. I told her I didn't feel like talking so we lay there in my bed and cried. I wanted to tell her but I was afraid she would tell my parents, I stopped going to counselling right after that. I told my mom I didn't need to go anymore. Nine days later, my parents found out what had happened. They were furious with me that they found out from someone else other than me. I was mad that they even found out. They took me to the emergency room to get tested for STDs. They made me talk to the cops when I just wanted to go hide from the world. He ended up walking free and didn't get charged for anything because he took a lie detector test and passed. That's when people started to not believe me. He and his friends would text me saying I made his life hell and to go die. His fiancée texted me saying that I was mad about him having sex with me and leaving so I made up something that didn't happen. I had some people say I provoked him and led him on. After that I started cutting again and I started shutting people out.

My senior year started off to an okay start. I was so excited to finally almost be done with school. I became really good friends with this girl who was a year younger than me and I was becoming more open about things. We helped each other through a lot. But one day she all of a sudden turned on me. She texted me telling me to cut myself and kill myself because nobody would care. One of my friends found out that I was cutting myself and she went through a similar situation. So one day she went in and talked to the counsellor and he called me into his office. At that point I wanted to stop. He told me I had to tell my parents, I was terrified. I decided to tell them anyways. They were concerned. I tried to stop, but I didn't feel like I could. I started to believe that this is just how I'm supposed to be.

Three days before Christmas break I had some guy texting me, not knowing where he got my number. He was telling me to go kill myself and that not one person would even care. At this point I decided I was done with just sitting back and taking other people's words, so I attempted to defend myself. I showed my counsellor the texts and the things he was telling me. My counsellor told me that because I texted back there was nothing he could do about it. I was hurt. I became more depressed than ever. I started self-medicating. I would pour alcohol in a water bottle and drink it at school just to get me through the day. I started cutting more and more frequently.

Once I graduated high school, I was relieved, but the messages didn't ever stop. I was getting messages telling me to slit my wrists so deep that I'd bleed out. One week before Thanksgiving of 2013 I cut three times on my arm. They were so deep that they needed stitches. My parents were out of town for Thanksgiving, so they weren't home. My oldest sister was scared at that moment. In the emergency room they had me make up a safety plan with a caseworker. I wasn't allowed to go sleep in my own room, I couldn't go on any social media sites for triggering purposes, and I wasn't allowed to be left by myself. I was diagnosed with major depression and anxiety disorder. I was prescribed medication to help stabilize my moods but I didn't think they helped me. They ended up just taking me off my medication all together.

After going to the emergency room, I tried really hard to stop cutting and stick to my safety plan. But two weeks later I was alone at home and ended up cutting again. I texted my sister in law because I was sure it needed medical attention. I went back to the emergency room for more stitches. I was really afraid of how my family was going to react. My oldest sister was really mad with me. When my parents got back, I had to tell them about both visits to the emergency room. My oldest sister beat me to it and told them for me. My mom asked me why they didn't admit me to the behavioural unit and my sister told her that they said I did it for attention. I got mad because that is not what they said. I told them they didn't admit me because it wasn't a suicide attempt. Of course they didn't believe me though. At home, I got told things from I look ugly with all the scars that I have on my body to being offered a blade to cut myself with.

I ended up packing my stuff and moving out with other family members to get help with my recovery. There was one rule at their place, no cutting. I was really scared to stop. After doing it for five years I didn't

51

think I was going to ever know how not to cut. While I was working on myself and stay in recovery I messaged my family and explained why I did what I did. I now know the reason why they said the things they did was because they didn't understand it and didn't know how to take it. After two months without cutting I moved back into my parents house. I got a job to keep myself busy.

Still to this day I have days where I don't know whether to stay in recovery or go back to my old habits. I know going back isn't an option but I'm going to deal with it for the rest of my life. People think once you're in recovery for a while that you're fixed, that's not true. I'm never really going to be fixed. I'm going to have my good days and my bad days, but my recovery doesn't have a day off. I was not only hurting myself but I was hurting everyone around me.

The hardest part of my recovery was learning and believing that I'm worth recovery. No one deserves to be bullied. I always used to wonder why other people said what they did. I don't really think I'll ever have the answer to that, but I do believe that a bully bullies because they're either being bullied or something terrible is going on in their lives.

This is my story of how I survived being bullied.

TANYA

I would like to say that my childhood was easy. I would like to have memories of wonderful things that I could bring to mind to comfort me on days that things are not going so well. Granted, I do have a few of those and I treasure them dearly. More so, though, are the things that haunt me about my tender years that make a bad day even worse. I do not believe that I will ever forget the things that have happened to me, but I have tried very hard to get over them and move on.

At the beginning of my teenage years, my parents had a male friend whom they used to spend a considerable amount of time with. I had met this man many times and knew him as well as a young teenager could know an adult, or so I thought. Looking back, I remember an uneasiness that would come over me when I was alone with this man, but I could not explain it to myself, much less to anyone else.

The beginning of February 1978, I happened to be home from school as I was ill. About two o'clock in the afternoon, an unannounced and unexpected vehicle pulled into the yard. It was this "friend". At first he claimed to be concerned that I was unwell and decided to come and check on me at the request of my mother. He had popped in where she worked and found out I was home ill. He knew because of her key position she could not leave work unless it was an emergency. I had no reason to doubt this because in my mind adults did not lie about things like that.

I remember the day well. It was horribly cold and windy outside. The house seemed eerily noisy with the boards cracking in the cold. The beautiful sunshine misled many that dared to venture outside in the cold wind. When this man entered the house, I immediately got that uneasy feeling. It was like knowing something awful was going to happen, but not quite being able to put your finger on exactly what that may be.

He entered the kitchen and sat down. I asked him if he would like some coffee, as the coffee pot in our home was always on the go. There was no set time for coffee breaks in our life. Whenever the cup was empty, or the urge struck, it was always there waiting to fulfil the desire. After pouring a coffee, I brought two cups to the table. As I turned to go and get the sugar and some spoons, I felt hands grab me from behind. Before I could say anything, he had his hands and his lips everywhere. I wanted to vomit. I was an innocent child and I still treasured my first kiss three years earlier from a young man only a year older than I was. There was something horribly wrong with this situation. I tried to push him away. I tried to tell him to stop. My muffled voice tried to scream to the silent house, but was covered by his rough and forceful kisses. It seemed like forever, but in reality it was about ten minutes until he pushed me toward the living room. I remember being not so gently tripped onto the floor and before I could get up, he had his pants unfastened. I had never seen a man naked before. It was a very frightening thing. He grabbed me by my hair and brought my face close to his erect penis. I remember him saying to me, "If you are going to be my girl, you are going to have to learn how to suck cock." He opened my mouth by forcing himself past my lips. I had no idea what was happening. I felt sick. He wouldn't stop and started ramming his hips back and forth while holding tight to my hair so I couldn't escape. I tried to push him away from me, wildly looking around for anything I could use as a weapon to make him stop. The only thing I could see out of the corner of my eye was the heavy glass bowl that sat on the coffee table, but it was too far out of my reach to be of any help. The strangest things happen when you are in a bad situation. I remember thinking to myself, that I couldn't use that bowl because it was my mother's favourite and I would catch hell for breaking it. Then I would have to explain what had happened. My mind would not let me even explain what was happening to myself, never mind to anyone else.

When he had had enough making me "learn" how to please him with my mouth, he held my hands behind my back and pinned my legs down with his. He took my pants and underwear off and tossed them beside me. I tried to fight. I wriggled hard and tried to bite and scratch him to make him let go of me. He just laughed and said he liked a girl with spirit. He spread my legs apart and rammed himself into me, ripping away my innocence. His hand was clamped tightly over my mouth, so I couldn't bite him or scream out in pain. I just gave up at that point. I laid there with tears running down my face as he continued until he was finished. He was a big man in more ways than one and he hurt me terribly. It was easy to hide the blood as I was old enough to have periods by that time and nobody ever questioned my moodiness or the products wrapped in the trash. Between my mood swings and emotional upheaval it was pretty obvious who was having their time of the month.

I do not remember him leaving the house. The last thing I remember was this heavy weight being lifted off me and the burning pain after he had withdrawn from my now broken body. It was pretty easy to conceal what

55

had happened to me that terrible day. I was sick, home from school, and my family knew that. I don't suppose it was a shock for them to find me bent over the toilet vomiting and crying when they came home. I had always had a horrible time with my periods. I was usually in a lot of pain, violently ill and vomiting until things calmed down. It was a pretty good cover for what had happened to me. It seemed relatively normal to my family members who just gave me my space and left me alone. I was so ashamed and afraid that I could not tell anyone but my best friend at school. She held me when I cried while telling her what had happened. She offered me friendship and concern when I couldn't tell anyone else. I trusted her with my deepest and darkest secret and she has never violated that trust. I will forever be grateful to her and her support during that terrible time.

I began to watch when I went places I had seen him before this happened so that I could make sure there was no more contact because I truly do not know if I could have gone through that again. My family started noticing I acted a little odd when they talked about this friend. My best friend supplied me with a pocketknife to carry in my purse in case I should meet up with him again. She offered to castrate him for me if I couldn't do it myself. We joked about that many times because her humour seemed to help me get past my worst moments and level out as well as I could emotionally.

It took me a long time before I could tell the events of that day to anyone but my best friend. When I did try I was glared at with a look of disbelief or disgust. I think that hurt me worse than the day I was raped. About a year afterward, I met up with a girl at school who asked me if I knew this man. I told her that he was a friend of my family. She warned me to be very careful and to never be alone with him. I still couldn't reveal my secret, so I played dumb and asked her why. She told me that he had been friends with her mother, for a time, and had raped her sister in her mother's absence. She told me that he had threatened her that she was next and pulled a knife out of her purse to show me what was waiting for him if he should return to fulfill his threat. By the time she made the comment about him returning, I had tears running down my face. She kept asking me what was wrong. I couldn't answer. I simply reached into my purse and pulled my knife out and held it out for her to see. I didn't have to tell her, she already knew. She later told me that it was the same look her sister had after he raped her. She told me that her mother wanted to press charges, but that her sister was too ashamed and begged her mother not to.

This was a long time before the no tolerance laws that are in place now. She went on to tell me how her sister said, the damage is done, so what will being in the middle of a legal mess achieve? I knew just how she felt. More embarrassment, more shame, more names, more horrible looks, no, it would achieve nothing. Plus the fact that if my own family didn't believe me, why would the police?

I was a lot older when the news broke about this man and how he had befriended many women, got money from them and had forced sexual intercourse with their daughters. There was a giant court case quite a while after it happened, although it seemed like it was yesterday. I finally had closure when it appeared in the newspaper that he had dropped dead. I remember that day very well. It was raining outside. It was cloudy and overcast but calm. I had sent my children off to school and then sat down with my ever-present cup of coffee and opened the paper. I read the article over three times to make sure I wasn't misreading things. He was dead.

The bastard who raped me was dead. He was gone. I went outside and cried and danced in that wonderful cleansing rain. I think my family thought I had gone insane, but it was so good. Life would be good again. No more fear of it ever happening again because he couldn't hurt me anymore. Yes, life would be good again, or would it? This is only a small look at the horrors of my life. One day I may write about the others, but for today, my coffee is fresh and hot, my tears have stopped and indeed, life is good.

PEBBLES

We have all heard of the terminology called "gender roles". We are all exposed to that phrase at some point or another; especially if you have taken a psychology or sociology class in high school or college. The thing is that here in America, no one talks to much about what roles we play when it comes to your race. When it comes to your race, whether it is white, Hispanic, or African American, what do you think your peers, family members, or your coworkers expect of you socially? Of course the word stereotype is heard all over the newspapers, but we never get into detail about what is expected of us depending on what race we are. It is an unspoken truth that no one frankly talks about it outside of the home. After my years in middle school, it truly gave me something to think about.

I was born in Massachusetts but for the most part grew up in Virginia due to moving there when I was six. My family moved around a lot. We never could stay in one neighbourhood for more than three years. This was mostly due to never having enough money and barely making ends meet. From fifth grade to eighth I lived at the oceanfront. The area was filled with laid-back kids who were into music, skateboarding, and enjoying the outdoors. Although I was very quiet, and often kept to myself, I fit right in and did make friends. I was never one to conform to what people wanted me to do and was always different from other African American girls. I loved rock music since I was seven. It was a strong interest that tended to baffle a lot of family members who expected me to listen to "black music". As a result, my taste in clothing was also quite different being that I loved to wear T-shirts sporting those of prevalent rock bands and rugged Converses with wild shoelaces.

The time came when I had to move away again from the comfort of my environment at the oceanfront. I really hated to move since I was at the tail end of my eighth grade year. We ended up moving into a house further inland three months before my eighth grade year was over. It was once again time for me to say goodbye to another school, classmates and teachers that I was familiar with, and most importantly to the friends I had made.

The first day at a new school is always nerve wracking for any teenager. The vulnerability and anxiety can be overwhelming for anyone. During lunch, I sat by myself and kept the yearbook from my previous school with me. It was then that it happened, when everything changed in my frame of thinking for the rest of my life. I happened to look up and a group of schoolgirls were laughing uncontrollably at me. One of the girls in the group informed me that they were laughing and asked if I was going to do something about it. I promptly told her no and continued to look down to avoid eye contact. From then on out, these girls seemed to be everywhere I went. I faced consistent criticism, even when switching classes in the hallways. They laughed at my T-shirts, my sneakers, my love of rock, the type of jeans I wore. I guess I figured if I ignored them, it would go away. I wasn't one to fight, and at that time never really had the urge to unless it was absolutely necessary.

However, every day I woke up for school, the agony of having to face these girls teasing all the time was torturing to me. I was so uncomfortable going to school and dealing with the fact of being taunted due to the way I dressed or what my interests were. Countless times when my alarm would go off before school, I would lie in the bed and stare ahead feeling unable to get up. Wondering for at least fifteen minutes if I should just feign sickness to avoid going in. Every now and again at school, I would deal with a sporadic person here or there giving me some kind of grief about my shirt. Or I would deal with the stares, but I always would do my best to avoid eye contact.

I did express my concerns to my parents, but at that time it seemed as if they didn't understand to the fullest how bad I felt. Their solution was to fight back and I was even granted permission to hit them to make them back off. I just couldn't get myself to do that. It seemed as if that was what they were looking for. I never even thought to tell a teacher. I do, however, remember one teacher intervening when a girl was asking me questions about what rock groups I listened to. I never thought of it then, but he must have seen all that was going on. About a month later, he pulled me out of the class and put me into one of his Advanced Science courses. He felt I was a very good student and could learn more in that class. Moving into the Advanced Science course did make my life a little easier due to the fact that it was at a different time slot. A lot of the girls were not around during that time, so in a way it threw things off.

I couldn't help but notice that the people that gave me a hard time with my listening to rock music were African American. I say this because I think in their minds or in a lot of people's minds that is not what is expected of me as an African American girl. Anything outside of rap or R &

B, would put me in the category of a "cornball" as one person called me in gym class. It stings, and it is a silly concept, but for the most part true. I still listen to rock and since I have become an adult have been to some rock concerts. I had to learn though, to never change for anyone even if they are against it. Never conform to what society wants you to because if you do, you will never be happy. Your true friends and whomever you fall in love with will always respect you for who you are.

CASIA

What can I say? When it came to bullying I got lucky. What I went through wasn't as severe as what others faced. My parents stayed together until cancer took my mom. There was no abuse at home. My sister and I fought, but nothing more than the usual sibling stuff. My grandparents are still together, both sets. I was part of a strong faith community. I knew who I was and I could just keep going through the bullying. That doesn't mean it didn't hurt.

The bullying started in the sixth grade. Kids' stuff, mostly, supposed to be normal and harmless. We were a small class – 11 girls and 1 boy. By this time I knew I interacted better with boys than with girls, and with adults better than my peers. But, it's the gender issue that arose here. Because I was friends with the only boy in class, and because I hung out with some of the boys a year younger than me, I got a lot of, "You like so-and-so!" It didn't so much hurt as make me feel awkward.

Junior high only enforced that awkwardness. More than learning math or science, those years I learned that I was different. I went to a private school to learn about religion, not because it would look good on my school record or because the education was better. I actually like to read and immersed myself in a world of fantasy. I don't remember a single other student mentioning that they read for fun. I was already writing by that age, again, the only one.

Every difference was noted and cruelly pointed out to me at every turn, teaching me that being different got you picked on. But I couldn't be anyone else. I still have trouble fitting in because I find it hard to make those little personality changes that allow people to interact with lots of different people. I am me and I can't be anyone else, I can't even be just a part of me and leave the rest locked away.

In high school, I fell in with a group of people who said they accepted me. Some of them were friends, the rest were just people to sit at a lunch table with. Some of them were card buddies and we played Crazy Eights, Poker, Cheat, and Blackjack on our spares. Some of them were friends of friends and we would make small talk or do homework together when there was no one else to hang out with. But I still didn't fit in the way others seemed to.

There was one group that really didn't like me. Now, I wore braces in high school and the girls called me Ducky because my upper lip stuck out because of the braces and my overbite. It hurt when they'd pass and yell, "How's it going Ducky?" and laugh. Telling them it hurt wouldn't have helped. We tell our kids this lie that all they have to do is say, "I don't like that, please stop," but it doesn't work, and I'll tell you why.

"It's just a joke." Or maybe you heard, "I was just joking." Or the ever popular, "Can't you take a joke?"

If you take it, you're an easy target. If you throw a fit, you're entertainment. If you stand up and say "Stop" then you're humourless and out of touch. They don't stop. They don't stop until they break you. And when kids snap they sit there, dumbfounded, saying "It was just a joke, we didn't mean it."

The one time I fought back, I became the bad guy. This girl walked by and said, "How's it going Ducky?" and I said, "I'm great, how are you, Cow?" I was the bad guy. I was picking on her for her weight. I was rude. I was mean. Yeah, right.

When I did make a friend, other girls tried to drive a wedge between us. They basically kidnapped my friend and tried to "brainwash" her into not being my friend anymore. Turns out one of those two became one of my best friends and one of the few who I still talk to, ten years after graduating, and she still apologizes.

When she apologizes I laugh it off. It doesn't matter anymore. It was ten years ago.

Ten years ago, it hurt. It was awful; sitting alone in a hallway, knowing that people thought you weren't worth the gift of friendship. But what can you do?

This same girl who later became my friend once took something from me. It wasn't really stealing since I saw her take it and knew she had it. The point was that she wouldn't give it back. It was a stuffed black panther, about four or five inches tall and maybe nine inches long. My boyfriend had bought it for me for no reason at all and it was the first time any boy had ever done that. At that moment that silly, cheap, little panther meant everything to me. She took it from me and refused to give it back, so I jabbed her in the leg with my pen. I'm not proud to admit that, it wasn't a good thing to do. But she just wouldn't give it back.

And after I jabbed her I was the bad guy. What I had done had hurt this girl. Taking the cat was just a joke. No one got hurt.

No one took into account my feelings. No one acknowledged the pain I was put through. If it's not visible, like a dot of ink on your thigh, it's not real. It's just a joke.

There were evenings when I would get home and stop at the far end of the driveway. I would put the car in park and sit there. I wanted to turn the car around and drive. I had a few grand and a car. How far could I get? I didn't know, but I wanted to run. I wanted to drive and keep driving until I broke down or until the cops found me and dragged me home.

I never did, but I wanted to.

That pain builds up inside of you, and if you don't try to kill the pain, it is still there. It makes it hard to trust people. It makes it hard to make friends. It makes it hard to love. You want to shut the whole world out and never ever let anyone close enough to you to hurt you. And it just keeps building and building until it's beyond overwhelming. I know because my chest is tightening as I type this. I see the faces of my tormentors. I know their names. I remember being afraid of the change room or of walking down 'Jock Hallway' alone.

But at the end of the day I left all the bullying behind. Now the bullying follows kids everywhere. There is no escape. And teens are vicious, ruthless, relentless predators.

Bullying is moving out of the schools and onto the internet. Teens don't call each other names in the hallways and the change rooms; they send them via text message and on social media. But the excuse is still the same.

"It was just a joke."

It's not a joke. It's not funny.

I loved school. If I had the money I'd be a career student. I love books, fiction and non-fiction alike. I love to learn. I love to debate and argue just as much as I love to sit back and listen and take it all in. I have always been like that, but by senior year all I wanted was to be out of high school. I wanted it to be over. I wanted to be away from all the childish stink and stupid drama. The bullying almost robbed me of my love of learning.

And I did get out. I went on to the University of Manitoba and the University of Winnipeg. I got a BA in English and History. I got a diploma certifying me as an Educational Assistant. I got married (yes, to the boy who bought me the panther, and yes, I still have it) and had two kids. I survived.

I want to end with a quote from my novel, *"Nothing, Everything, Nothing."* One of my characters, Brandon, does a presentation on cyber bullying after his best friend is driven to attempt suicide by her peers and this is his summary.

Most of you looked offended and horrified when I told the stories of Amanda Todd and Megan Meier. But of the eighteen people in this class twelve of them posted rude, insulting, or suggestive comments on the photos Lance posted. Twelve of you, at least, helped push Molly to suicide.

In summary: bullying isn't a joke, we can't dismiss it. It is normal, ordinary teens who are the bullies, and the victims. Teens need to be held accountable for their words and actions, in school, on the streets, and online. If we are not, more of us will commit suicide. More of us will die.

***

Casia Schreyer is an author from southeastern Manitoba. Nothing, Everything, Nothing is her first young adult novel and her first self-published novel. Her short story, "We Will Not Go Quietly" was recently featured in the science-fiction anthology Of Stars and Science: Tales of the Multiverse.

Myth #6

"There have always been bullies and there always will be."

Reality

By working together as parents, teachers and students we have the power to change things and create a better future for our children. As a leading expert, Shelley Hymel, says, "It takes a whole nation to change a culture". Let's work together to change attitudes about bullying. After all, bullying is not a discipline issue - it is a teaching moment.

CHRISTOPHER

I write to you as an ambassador of change, not just as a human being, but as someone who is seeking your support with grace and humility from the depths of my life, I seek for you to read this sincerely from the depths of your life and from your heart:

I am a survivor of a horrific nightmare that now is being addressed in the social consciousness... bullying.

I know about bullying because I have endured this due to a mental challenge that I have called infantile autism. Autism is a lifelong challenge that affects several regions of the brain in particular. The first time I was affected by bullying, was when someone whipped me with a rubber snake, causing red welts all over my back and shoulders. When my mother saw the welts, she asked me who did this, at this time, the kind of autism that I had, didn't give me the language abilities to address me being affected by bullying of such a scale, I told her who did it and my mother came on the bus to address the person who had the snake and asked to give it to her and more. I thought that was just the end of this, but I was wrong.

As I grew older, the bullying got worse and worse, some people called me names such as "Retarded", "Slow", etc. Some even made fun of me trying to have a lady in my life, and one in particular cut my ponytail off when I was trying to grow one, and I couldn't even tell the teachers who it was, and it hurt so bad, till finally I yelled. I even busted out crying to mom, it took some time, but finally I told the teachers what was going on. I was trying to live my life, but the bullies were trying to destroy my life, but they failed in doing so.

I was one among the lucky ones who had the support of teachers, peers and those who cared and I also refused to hear the word "Surrender". Some of the bullies who even taunted and teased me have approached me to ask for the forgiveness and atonement of the slanderous errors they had endured upon me. When I was older, I felt that there was no one (as far as I can recall) that spoke out for those with challenges, I ran for the NJ assembly seat as the first person with autism on a political party ticket, and won 15% of the vote from the people. Tragically though, the nightmare that is bullying has reached levels that are considered criminal and worse, in fact, according to the website: Stompoutbullying.org the statistics are totally alarming and it is clear evidence that something MUST and SHOULD be done:

- 1 out of 4 kids is bullied
- 9 out of 10 LGBT students experienced harassment at school
- Child and teen Bullying and Cyber bullying are at an all-time high
- Some kids are so tormented that suicide has become an alternative for them

As many as 160,000 students may stay home on any given day because they're afraid of their bullies and/or they just can't take the pain anymore. 43% fear harassment in the bathroom at school
A poll of teens ages 12-17 proved that they think violence increased at their schools

282,000 students are physically attacked in secondary schools each month. More youth violence occurs on school grounds as opposed to on the way to school.

That is why as an advocate, it was my immense good fortune to create one of the toughest anti-bullying Bills in the nation along with Assemblywoman Valerie V. Huttle.

The recent stories of youth taking their own lives because of the bullying, harassment and cyber-bullying prompted me to become a voice for the voiceless. The names such as Tyler Clementi, Phoebe Prince, Jamey Rodemeyer and numerous others are the names of those who we shall never ever forget as long as we live.

This tragedy is growing and growing at such a rate that SOMETHING has to be done to protect the lives of our future leaders of change, justice, peace and more, regardless of gender preference and more, we must call upon our national and international leaders to make bullying and bully-cide deemed criminal and that the laws should be toughened for older youth who do mental and physical damage to the youth because of their gender preference, religion and more by facing a student court based on the school constitution and the laws in the constitution as well.

The youth of America have always gone to school to follow the three "R's": Reading, Writing, and Arithmetic, all the things that make going to school very important. The youth of America and the world are tired of living their life in fear and it is time to give them a voice to stand up against bullying without the usage of violence. There are those who feel they do not have a voice to speak up feel that they lose hope and cannot speak up for themselves because they are not taught how. So they need our help.

On a grassroots internet petition website called change.org, I have been collecting signatures to bring to Washington D.C. and to other leaders of the world to address this issue strongly and so far over 1,232 people have signed my petition at this website.

In conclusion, I am appealing you, all of you to come to sign my petition. Take a firm and united stand with me to address this crisis of significant urgency and tell our national and international leaders to hear the cries of the youth and help them sincerely, so one day, this law that can be passed, will not only be my testament to the great impact what one person can do, but what the world can do.

There are two people in my life (including my mom) among many who have been in my life and I have taken their quotes as my mantra to my mission, the first is John F. Kennedy who said in his inauguration speech in 1961, "And so my fellow citizens, ask not, what your country can do for you, ask what you can do for your country!" and to conclude my editorial is a quote from a Japanese Buddhist philosopher named Daisaku Ikeda who said, "A great human revolution in just a single individual will help achieve a change in the destiny of an entire nation and further will help achieve a change in the destiny of the entire human race." If one person can start that positive change in the world, then many, many, more can achieve what I have achieved in my 33 years upon this earth with such a challenge.

Your voices can be a part of history, and to make a message loud and clear. Every single night I got to sleep, I offer a sincere prayer from my heart that someone will step up and tell others and make a mission of mine closer to being successful and for all youth, regardless of sexual gender preference, religion, etc. can go to school in peace and safety, and it is our voices that can be possible.

Thank you for the opportunity to give me this platform to share my story and my mission. I can only pray and hope that my story has inspired you and inspired others to help those who feel alone, sad and more to let them know, "Someone is out there to help you and someone is out there to give you the voice you need!"

#YOUTH #JUSTICE #CAMPAIGN #HOPE

***

Sign the petition at:
www.change.org/petitions/give_the_youth_the_rights_for_justice_agai nst_bullies#

Myth #7

"Kids will be kids."

Reality

Bullying is a learned behaviour. Children may be imitating aggressive behaviour they have seen on television, in movies or at home. Research shows that 93% of video games reward violent behaviour. Additional findings show that 25% of boys aged 12 to 17 regularly visit gore and hate internet sites, but that media literacy classes decreased the boys' viewing of violence, as well as their acts of violence in the playground. It is important for adults to discuss violence in the media with youth, so they can learn how to keep it in context. There is a need to focus on changing attitudes toward violence.

CANDACE

The first rays of spring sun glistened on puddles of water and little blades of grass began to peep above the ground. It was May and I had just announced my intention to run for public office in the upcoming fall election. This was the start of what would be an exhausting six-month campaign. In the beginning, I was excited and filled with hope. My life has changed significantly since that first day... cue the criticism and hate.

I believe that God lets us experience struggle sometimes so that we have a testimony that will give others hope and encouragement. In sharing my experience with you, my goal is to do exactly that.

My experience on the campaign trail was far from pleasant. I had to deal with a lot of negative criticism and that wasn't easy. People began to question and criticize every aspect of my life. From my appearance, age, faith, and even my employment – it seemed anyone and everyone had something to say.

We have a tendency to judge and criticize others. Have you been criticized for putting yourself out there, voicing an unpopular opinion or for trying something new that you haven't quite mastered? Maybe you've been hurt when someone has said that you're too shy, too outspoken, too skinny, too fat, not cooperative, too motivated… the list goes on.

Over the course of my campaign, I openly shared my pro-life beliefs and said that I support abstinence. It's not easy to share an unpopular or controversial opinion. People don't often share or speak up about their personal beliefs or values. It's something they keep hidden because they are concerned about how people will perceive them. They're often worried about this thing I absolutely despise called "political correctness". I'm not ashamed of my views, but I found myself in the middle of a firestorm that made me question whether or not I should have said anything at all. Do you ever find yourself in a crisis of faith where you're questioning or doubting a decision you made?

Journalists began contacting me for interviews and I soon found my name on national headlines. I received thousands of comments on social media that were filled with hate. I learned just how rampant cruelty is. People would say things about how they wished my parents would have abstained from having me. Other comments started flooding my Newsfeeds like, "You're disgusting. Why haven't you been drop kicked into a big pile of shit?" and "Hey you ugly toad. When's your next live debate so I can show you that I don't need to hide behind a screen?" Some thought that I should be fired from my job. I even received death threats. The campaign manager of a candidate running for city council asked me not to make any comments about the candidate on social media as they were afraid I would hurt their campaign. The people I called "close friends" distanced themselves from me. They deleted me off of Facebook and stopped responding to my texts. I was asked to resign as Vice-President of a campus group I had proudly served over the past year. I quickly learned that using politics as a standard to base friendships on is like building a house on quicksand. I stumbled across one website that showed a picture of me in a bathing suit and in the comments section, men were posting sexually explicit comments.

If these people were hoping their vicious attacks with their words would hurt me, it worked. I felt alone, broken, and defeated. I felt sick to my stomach and my heart ached. I cried. There were some days when I just wanted to hide under the covers in the comfort of my bed. Do you ever feel like you just can't face the world or want to isolate yourself from everyone – even the people closest to you?

I'm thankful for the wonderful people in my life that stood with me in this challenging time and supported me. I'm very thankful for Michael Coren and Sun News Network for the opportunity I had to address the comments from people who were attacking me online. Sharing my story has been helpful and healing for me.

There are so many mean-spirited and hate filled people out there who get their thrills by making nasty comments. It's easy to attack and criticize someone while he or she is taking a risk like voicing an unpopular opinion. Cruelty is cheap. Technology and the Internet allow so many people to hide their identities and attack and criticize anonymously. These people have no concern about how their comments will make the person on the receiving end feel. If you are struggling, I hope that you will find the courage to reach out and ask for support. Whatever you may be going through, you don't have to face it alone. Sharing your story may be the bravest and most healing thing you do.

There are times in our lives when we will feel beaten down and discouraged. I can't even tell you how many times over the course of the campaign and even throughout my life that I've felt that way. Some people told me not to read the comments. Others told me not to take it personally or that I needed to "toughen up" and grow a thicker skin. Easier said than done.

I wear a necklace that has the words "daring greatly" engraved on it. There's a powerful quote by Theodore Roosevelt that you may be familiar with. It's better known as the Man in the Arena quote and it goes like this… "It's not the critic who counts. Not the man who points out how the strong man stumbles or where the doer of deeds could have done them better. The credit belongs to the person who is in the arena. Whose faces are marred with dust and sweat and blood. Who strives valiantly. Who at best knows in the end the triumph of high achievement and who at worst, if he fails, at least fails while daring greatly."

I've come to learn that the more you put yourself out there and take a stand for something you believe in, the more people will try to tear you down. You have to get used to it if you want to come off the sidelines and be in the arena. Don't waver from your values. You have a choice each day to be true to who you are and to your values. Go out in the arena. Stand fear in the face. Build up your courage.

You will face critics everywhere you go. There will be a lot of people that tell you who you're supposed to be or what you should be doing. There will be those who stand in seething jealousy. You may feel defeated or isolated. You may feel like you're standing alone. Reach out for support when you need it. More than anything, know that you are loved and that God places great value on you. Continue to dare greatly!

This book is a campfire of hope. As you continue to read the stories of others, my wish for you is that it creates a spark that will light up your soul with strength, hope, and encouragement.

***

No stranger to the political arena, Candace Maxymowich has shared her experience running for public office at twenty years old. She made national headlines for stating her support for abstinence and sharing her pro-life views. She received thousands of personal attacks on social media, including death threats. She has risen above the hate and shown that she is a fearless fighter who will not be intimated. In her desire to share her story, Candace is available for public speaking and media interview opportunities. Maxymowich has received numerous awards for her many contributions to her community, including the Queen Elizabeth II Diamond Jubilee Medal, the Manitoba Council on Aging Recognition Award, the Lieutenant Governor's Make a Difference Community Award, the Fred Douglas Foundation Humanitarian Award, and was a YWCA Young Woman of Distinction Award nominee.

EVAN WIENS

Unfortunately, like many people, I have experienced bullying in all shapes and sizes. All throughout elementary school I was teased and bullied for being overweight. I was also religiously bullied: in Grade 3, I remember being told by a peer that I was going to hell because I watched Harry Potter and did not attend church; this concerned me because I knew that this child's hurtful words were not coming from their own mind, but obviously from their parents'.

The most amount of bullying I have ever experienced, however, started in junior high and continued all throughout high school. This type of bullying was bred from homophobia, whether it was religiously fuelled or not. As early as Grade 7, I can remember being called a "fag" in the change room before gym class; this caused me to start changing in the bathroom instead. However, because my peers were wondering why I wasn't changing in the change room anymore, they found me in the bathroom and continued to harass me there. All of this triggered me to stop going to gym class altogether. Then, in Grade 9, when gym class became mandatory, I started doing gym outside of class so I could still get the credit. I did gym entirely out of class for all of high school, as well.

The homophobic bullying I experienced increased by a large amount towards the end of Grade 8 and throughout Grade 9. There were times when I would feel so judged and intimidated at school that I would fake a headache and call my dad to pick me up from school and bring me home. I specifically remember one time where I stepped outside to call my dad, and while I was on the phone with him, a student opened the door and yelled "You're gay!" at me. I couldn't believe that someone would go out of their way to actually open a door and yell hurtful words at someone.

Another explicit instance of bullying in Grade 9 resulted in me reporting the incident to the RCMP. Two male students in my grade created and posted a video on Facebook, which falsely depicted one of my male friends and I, performing fellatio on each other; hurtful and discriminatory words were used in the video. Hearing about this video being posted on Facebook made me feel even more humiliated than I already did every day at school. My mom and I went to the RCMP and tried to charge the students with cyber bullying and defamation of my character. The RCMP didn't charge them, but gave them a stern warning and forced them to apologize to me in person.

As a result of all this bullying, I started searching the internet to see if I could find any resources for bullied LGBT* youth. I came across the term "Gay-Straight Alliance" (GSA) several times and subsequently looked deeper into what exactly a GSA was; I was amazed at how great a GSA sounded! I quickly went to my school administration and asked them if it would be possible for me to start a GSA. They promptly shut down my request and told me that I should wait until I started high school the following year to try starting a GSA. Being naïve at the time, I listened to what they told me and finished Grade 9, trying hard to ignore the bullying.

Grade 10 came around and the bullying increased to a new, physical level. I walked down the halls and got shoved by the same student every single day. When it first started happening, considering the fact that my high school was very crowded, I thought he was just accidentally bumping into me. However, after it started happening in various hallways that clearly weren't very crowded, I knew something was wrong. He would shove me so hard some days that I was worried I'd have a bruise as a result. I began feeling too afraid to walk down the hallway alone or turn certain corners; I constantly asked my friends to walk with me because I felt too scared. I wanted to tell someone about what was going on, but I was too frightened.

In the fall of 2011, a month or so after I started Grade 10, a 14-year-old boy from Buffalo, NY, USA named Jamey Rodemeyer killed himself because he was being bullied so harshly at school for being gay. I learned of his suicide on social media because he was a huge fan of Lady Gaga, as was I. Gaga herself heard of Jamey's suicide and dedicated a performance of her song "Hair", a song about keeping your identity strong while being in high school, to him. His suicide really affected me on a personal level and I decided that enough was enough: no one should feel afraid to be themselves at school or take their own life because of who they are.

At this point, I went straight to my guidance counsellor and told him I wanted to start a GSA. He told me that I could start a GSA, which I was very happy about. However, there was a catch. He said that because a GSA was a "student-initiated group", it could not advertise it in any form other than by word of mouth. I found this to be a bit odd because other groups put up posters and made announcements, but I was so excited that I could finally start a GSA that I put advertising aside. I made a mistake by putting advertising aside because the newly made GSA was not attracting any members; only a few of my straight friends joined. It also didn't help that the space we were given to meet was a tiny (and I mean tiny) conference room at the back of the school library (we had to be "quiet" as well). After I told my counsellor that the space was too small and wouldn't work, he offered the GSA a new space to meet: a classroom at the back of the kitchens (my high school was a vocational school). I felt like the school wanted our group to be hidden, which I didn't think was right at all. However, I was too afraid to stand up and fight for a different space and proper advertising, so I gave up and formally dissolved the group. I didn't think my high school would ever have a GSA.

A year and a half later, in February 2013, everything changed. My province, my school, my life... they were never going to be the same. There was a lot of controversy in Steinbach surrounding the Manitoba government's proposed anti-bullying legislation, Bill 18. I noticed that my local MLA, Kelvin Goertzen, along with Southland Community Church and Steinbach Christian High School, were all heavily opposing and voicing their opinions on Bill 18. Infuriated by their bigoted opposition, I decided that I would give it another go at starting a GSA at my high school; this time, there would be media attention. I didn't have to think too long about whether to get media involved or not; it just felt like the right thing to do. I emailed CBC and CTV on February 27, 2013 and told them about how I tried to start a GSA a year and a half prior and now wanted to try again. They wanted to do a story on me and came to Steinbach the following day. Interviews were conducted and I was featured in the local news on TV that evening. Little did I know that these few interviews would be a gateway into a whole new world of media attention for me. About a week later, during more interviews outside of my school, students walking by yelling gay slurs and jokes at me while the cameras rolled. This was quite a humiliating moment for me and it felt all too similar to when the student in Grade 9 shouted harmful words at me when I was on the phone with my dad.

A few weeks later, I had an interview with The Globe and Mail. My story was featured on the side column of the front page. After this, I completely lost track of the amount of interviews and events that followed. I did not expect my story to explode that largely across the country. I began receiving many letters of support at my school from all over Canada; I even received one from Minnesota! I also received a supportive email from Rick Mercer and tweets from George Stroumboulopoulos; that definitely felt great. I got into contact with Nancy Allan, Manitoba's education minister at the time and proposer of Bill 18, and formed a very special relationship with her. We became "partners in crime", if you'd like to call it that. I'm very thankful to this day for our friendship and she continues to be an inspiring force in my life.

Finally, a few weeks after my story went national, it was time to meet with the Hanover School Division (HSD) board of trustees. I had to meet with them to try and convince them to allow GSA advertising. They argued that it would be easier to wait until Bill 18 passed to allow advertising; I countered that argument by explaining that HSD could set an example to the rest of the province by allowing GSA advertising ahead of the bill passing. I also explained that it may take months for Bill 18 to pass (which was true, because it only passed in September 2013). On April 3, 2013, a day after I met with the board, I was told that I was successful in changing their policy on GSA advertising and that any GSA in the school division may now advertise the same as any other student-initiated group. It took a while for this excitement to sink in because of the fact that I had interviews waiting for me when I left the HSD office that day. It felt so amazing, though, to have actually made a difference in my school division.

After it was all over and I was allowed to advertise the GSA, it felt very rewarding. It also felt very scary because now I was a public figure. I was no longer "Evan Wiens, gay student fighting for the right to advertise a GSA". I was now "Evan Wiens, a gay student who fought for and won the right to advertise a GSA". I was invited to speak at multiple events and became sort of a poster teen for Bill 18. I will admit, I enjoyed the spotlight, but it took quite a large emotional toll on me. I was close to failing some classes at school, I didn't have much of a social life, and I generally felt as though I couldn't quite focus properly on what was going on in my life.

More than a year later, in October 2014, I'm able to look back on it all and take in the whirlwind that occurred in my life in those few months. I'm very proud of what I did at my high school. Our GSA met every single week after we won advertising rights, and we attracted a significant number of new students. We held two bake sales, which both raised over $600 that was donated to local charities. We hung out, we ate food, we laughed, and we conversed. I'm proud to say that now, after I've graduated, the GSA is still active, with many more events planned this year that I will be happy to be involved with.

Luckily, the bullying died down for me. I think that people caught on to my, "I don't care what you think about me," attitude I always portrayed and didn't find a point in picking on me. I know that it isn't easy to wake up one day and decide you're not going to listen to what anyone says negatively about you, but doing so really helped me in gaining better self-esteem and fighting off the bullies. It's hard to stay strong. It's hard to think you can create change. But you have to remember to stay true to your identity, love yourself (even on the bad days), and know that you can do anything when you put your mind to it and not give up. Positivity will always outweigh negativity. *Always.*

JENNA NICKIE

On September 25, 2014 my 10-year-old son, hung himself. I walked in on him. I actually interrupted him. Had I not walked in when I did, this story would have a much different ending. I would be burying my son. It would have been the heaviest 70 lbs I would ever lift.

He has been bullied at school since we moved to Carlyle, Saskatchewan three years ago. The first year I went to the school, talked to the principal and the vice-principal to no avail. I gave my son permission to defend himself from the kid who sat on his chest while they were on the playground and choked him. My boy was going to get an out of school suspension for dropping the kid who is twice his size, while the kid who was choking my boy, got an in school suspension.

I got Breck into counselling in the area, to help him deal with a new town, a new home, a new school, and that he was being bullied. Breck was still being bullied by the older kids in the school, so I started going to the parents because the school wouldn't help me. The last time my boy had mentioned anyone bullying him was November 20, 2012....almost 2 years ago!

I kept asking how the boys were at school and he kept telling me they were better. They weren't. They were getting meaner because I was going to the parents now. At this time, my boy was also bullied by a teacher in the school, the reading resource teacher. He was told in front of his peer group that he wasn't a strong or confident reader, that good readers read like she does, among other insults. She planted a stupid seed when Breck was in her grade 2 class and watered it. My boy was reading at a grade 2 level, going into grade 4, he was stunted by this teacher who can read well. I went to the Principal about this teacher, again, nothing was done. So I dealt with her myself.

My son also became a bully. His grades were consistently not good and I was having to deal with the school 2-3 times a month because Breck is aggressive on the playground with kids, not staying on task in class, and being disruptive. I know what my boy is capable of and I was working with the school, something the school wouldn't do for me the previous years Breck was enrolled there. At this point I got myself into counselling, thinking it was something within our walls that was affecting my son and making him lash out.

Upon entering my boys' room and seeing his neck all red with abrasions and seeing the noose in his closet, I asked him if he tried to hang himself? He said he did. I asked him why he stopped? He said because I was coming. I asked him if I wouldn't have noticed and had left, what would he have done? He said he would've went back into the closet and finished. I asked him where he got the rope from? The garage, he pulled it in a week prior, he sat for a week on that rope and didn't say a word. I asked him where he got the idea from? He responded, "Robin Williams hung himself."

The knot was a slipknot, and it held my weight!! He wasn't messing around.

I took my boy to the Weyburn General Hospital, we were seen in the middle of the night by the on call physician. She was yawning, it was late. She asked Breck what happened, he said that he tried to kill himself. She asked how, he told her he hung himself. She asked (in a condescending tone) "With what? A shoe lace?"

At which point I pulled out the rope. She spent two minutes with my boy and told me he wasn't depressed. I didn't get a chance to say anything at all. She then said, "You do realize that Social Services is going to come now."

Right in front of my boy, who literally shut down and was scared that they would take him from me, he needed help and just wanted to go home from this point on. I told him that they could try! But I would fight for him! The on call physician called a psychologist and we were admitted.

I was his suicide watch, in a room with so many cords and my boy who tried to hang himself. At 9 a.m. on September 26, the psychologist came to see Breck. He told the psychologist what he wanted to hear, "I won't do that again, I don't want to die, life isn't that bad." He was still scared they would take him from me.

The psychologist said he thought Breck was alright and would pass this along to the doctor who admitted us. The on call physician did not come to see us. I had legitimate concerns, there needed to be an action plan, the numbers I could call if I needed them! Nothing. She gave the nurses instructions to give us our discharge papers when Breck was ready to go. My 10 year old who had just tried to kill himself and was now deathly afraid Social Services was going to take him from me, was in charge of when he went home.

We came home the same afternoon. My partner and I cleaned out his room of anything that he could harm himself with. Breck showered. We were going to relax as much as possible. I moved a mattress into our room, I was scared to have him sleep in his room alone. The night went on.

Breck started crying, I asked him what was wrong. He said he was sad about what he did. I told him that was good, that means he wants to live . He started sobbing! I hugged him and asked him why he was crying harder. He told me he was sad that he didn't die. My heart broke again for the second time in as many days. Despite the doctor's declaration that my son wasn't depressed, he was! And it was way bigger than me!

Lucky for me and for my son, I have great friends that are able to be my voice of reason and tell me things that I might not want to hear! I was in crisis and I couldn't think properly. I hadn't slept in 72 hours because I was scared I would miss something and wake up and find my child dead.

We went to Saskatoon. Breck received the care and the help he needed. I have reported the doctor in Weyburn. I have gone to the school board and guess who is the superintendent? The principal who wouldn't help me for the last two years! She wouldn't help me then! So I went above her head and got her boss down here to Carlyle!

I have been in touch with the RCMP. I have gotten the ball rolling. I called some other parents, whose kids I know are being bullied so they can come forward and help their kids. Four different sets of parents have declined! Their reasons when asked were (and I quote), "I still have to work here." "We can't because of my husbands job."

Adults are scared of other adults...adults bullying adults!! And we wonder why our kids are bullied or bullies.

It rests with me. I will advocate for every child in Carlyle, who is being bullied! Not just for my son, but for everyone's kids. I have blown the school out of the water in terms of the teachers that bully the students, that they are quick to jump down Breck's throat because I'm not the "Lil Johnny would never" parent. They are perfectly clear that I'm not going away.

The school board is implementing a "Respect Ed" program at the high school. They have made it a mandatory course for the elementary school, despite the fact that it's for Grades 7 and up. The RCMP are also going to ALL the schools in the area and doing presentations.

I am not done here. You will know when I'm done, the smoke will clear and Carlyle will be left picking up its pieces of its facade it once called life. I don't give a rats ass what anyone thinks of me, least of all the fakes down here, I have nothing to lose...but my son! I almost missed it, NEVER AGAIN!

Talk to your kids! Help them! They need you!

Myth #7

"Kids will be kids."

Reality

Bullying is a learned behaviour. Children may be imitating aggressive behaviour they have seen on television, in movies or at home. Research shows that 93% of video games reward violent behaviour.

Additional findings show that 25% of boys aged 12 to 17 regularly visit gore and hate internet sites, but that media literacy classes decreased the boys' viewing of violence, as well as their acts of violence in the playground. It is important for adults to discuss violence in the media with youth, so they can learn how to keep it in context. There is a need to focus on changing attitudes toward violence.

LEAH PARSONS

Some days you wake up and you just want it to be a dream... just want your life back... just want to receive that text that says, "Morning Momma, what are you up to? Can you give me a drive?" This is how I have felt since the day I discovered the light of my life, my daughter, had taken her life.

The person Heather once was all changed one dreaded night in November 2011. She went with a friend to another's home. In that home, she was raped by four young boys... one of those boys took a photo of her being raped and decided it would be fun to distribute the photo to everyone in Heather's school and community where it quickly went viral. Because the boys already had a "slut" story, the victim of the rape Heather was considered a 'slut'. This day changed the lives of our family forever. I stopped working that very day and we have all been on this journey of emotional turmoil ever since.

My daughter was suddenly shunned by almost everyone she knew, the harassment was so bad she had to move out of her own community to try to start anew in Halifax. She struggled emotionally with depression and anger. Her thoughts of suicide began and fearing for her life, she placed herself in a hospital in an attempt to get help. She stayed there for almost 6 weeks. The bullying continued, her friends were not supportive. She needed a friend and eventually along the way a few new friends came along and a few old friends came forward. Heather then moved back to Dartmouth, always with the concern of what will be said about her, said to her. Again, she was the one raped, yet she was the victim being victimized over and over again.

One year later the police concluded their investigation to state that it comes down to, "he said, she said" they believed the boys raped her but the proof in a court of law was difficult to gather. The bullying never stopped, but she learned to keep her head high and surrounded herself with the ones who truly cared. I will have eternal gratitude for her friends; they are the ones she leaned on for strength and courage.

We lived that nightmare for seventeen months. Until she couldn't deal with it any longer.

I would always try to teach Heather to "rise above" to "never lower yourself to their level". If they know they are getting to you, then they win. On and on our talks went about the way teenagers treat each other. I would also try to let her know that what happens to you does not define you. To try to not let them have the power over you psychologically by taking up room in your mind. These words of wisdom were the very ones my mom and dad taught us and it's hard to grasp as a teenager full of torment, anger and sadness.

The week before she died, she was having lots of mood swings and her friends bore the brunt of it, but on Thursday, April 4 she had a great day, and even made plans for the weekend. However, later that evening she had an outburst, acted on that impulse and locked herself in the bathroom. And to stop any rumours from spreading. She acted on an impulse, but I truly in my heart of hearts do not feel she meant to kill herself. By the time

I broke into the bathroom it was too late. My beautiful girl had hung herself and was rushed to the hospital where she remained until we turned off life support on April 7, 2013.

People were so very cruel to her. Heather is gone today because four boys thought that raping a 15-year-old girl was okay. They thought distributing a photo to ruin her spirit and reputation would be fun. All the bullying and messaging and harassment that never lets up are also to blame. Lastly, the justice system failed her. Those are the people who took the life of my beautiful girl. Heather stood up for others, showed compassion to animals and people. She was an amazing artist. She made my life complete. When Heather was born I dedicated everything to her and promised her the world. Others in this world took that away from her.

Of course I am beyond devastated and often I still expect Heather to burst through that door and say, "Hey Mama!". Other times, tears just overwhelm me and I feel struck by a sudden surge of profound sadness. However, knowing that other people care about what happened to Heather has given me a sense of hope and it feels like people want to know Heather.

I am honouring Heather by remembering her determination to heal, her resilient spirit, her love of life. It's easy to get overwhelmed by thoughts of how she was wronged, how much pain she endured, how anger and sadness and fear consumed her in the months after she was sexually assaulted. She wasn't always this way. And even after being so hurt, betrayed by people she thought were friends, she was still trying every day to heal. Today I remember her life, her life force!

It's so ironic to me that we keep telling our children to speak out and tell people, school officials or police that they are being harassed (bullied is the term thrown around way too often) yet they don't want them or anyone to discuss suicide or suicide ideation.

95

I truly believe that many children speak out and telling people that they are being harassed online and in school. In turn, their parents start to advocate for them only to be told, "There is nothing we can do," or "We don't consider that bullying," or "If you go to the police it could get worse for your child."

What is the policy of each school? Where is the consistency? One of the recommendations of the school review was to tell an adult within the school and if that does not work tell someone else? That's the solution? We need to do more... a LOT more. Education and prevention are key, but in the meantime, we need to help the child in immediate danger - not months and months later when their self worth has crumbled.

Do you remember being a teen? How fragile your sense of self was in its initial development? Now imagine being a target of hatred and ridicule by everyone around you via social media. Isolation and loneliness soon become feelings of despair at a time when you were defining the person you would become. Kids are speaking out, but who is going to listen?

This world we live in, full of technology is very dangerous and it's so easy for a young person to join in and "target" someone by saying mean things via texting or sending online messages. We don't have to go far to see how cruel people can be. Have you seen the page Cutest Teens on Facebook? The damaging effects come fast and are debilitating to the person receiving it. It can happen to anyone and bringing someone's self-esteem down to a point where they don't want to live in this world anymore is outright cruelty.

Heather was once a confident, smart girl with the world at her fingertips. In the blink of an eye, one evening, a photo circulated, targeting her as a "slut" meant for some that she had no value as a person. She was now a "slut" even to those who knew her all her life. How can that happen so fast? She was already suffering, then to become the target of ridicule and harassment. She was so strong in her sense of identity and was brought down to her knees. She no longer wanted to live. This is not some character flaw, this is what harassment does to people. Do you really want to treat someone so bad that they question their very existence? This is not schoolyard jokes and jeers we are talking about. Not to diminish the bullying, but what I am discussing is social annihilation.

When you see this type of behaviour happening, I challenge you to not go along, do not be a follower. It's understandable. It is hard to stand up against others. Who wants to be the next "target"? No one wants to be put in that situation, but you can choose not to participate. You can choose to tell others. You don't have to take on the world, but maybe you can send the person being harassed a message saying what is happening is wrong. Pull them aside and tell them you support them? Don't let them feel all alone and isolated.

There are many ways to be an upstander and not a bystander. You could save a life!

Heather's legacy started pretty quickly. She has touched many lives. Her legacy is ensuring we do better, by helping others speak out when sexualised violence is seen or heard. She also inspires people to do better and to love themselves in the ebb and flow of life.

The goal, of Glen and me is to spread awareness through education and participation of the community. By inspiring people to become involved in the issues children are faced with. That is the desire to build the Heather Parson's Society. One day to open a facility where children get the support, encouragement and skills to cope with an ever-changing world.

***

On May 20, 2014, a Nova Scotia judge implemented a publication ban on the use of Heather's real name. Recently one of her alleged attackers plead guilty to charges of distribution of pornography. The Law clearly states that victims of child pornography cases must remain unnamed for their protection once a case is in court. The Parsons family has not been successful in their appeal to have the publication ban lifted, despite their argument that the case is known worldwide, and the victim is deceased. Nova Scotia media have got past the ban by using code. They call her Heather, which is her name spelt backwards.

Heather Anne Parsons was born December 9, 1995, in Halifax, Nova Scotia to Leah Parsons and Glen Canning. She died April 7, 2013, at the age of 17. Directly following Heather's death, her parents used social media to go public with her story, drawing attention both nationally and internationally.

New evidence emerged prompting the re-opening of the investigation and in August of 2013, two of the four boys were charged; one with the creation and distribution of child pornography and one with distribution of child pornography. No other charges were laid. The two boys charged are now adults; however, because their crime occurred when they were youths, their names are not able to be revealed in adherence with the Youth Offenders Act of Canada. The presentation of these charges is currently before the courts in Halifax.

The family's goal is to develop a Youth Centre in Cole Harbour in Memory of Heather. The focus of the Centre will be a safe haven for youth who may feel judged, rejected, or temporarily lost. For more information, visit www.raeoflight.com.

JADE

I was twelve! I was a healthy, happy, bubbly, kind and gentle natured girl, intelligent and loved learning, but that was all about to change! For a number of months leading up to the day that changed my life, I had been subjected to name calling, taunting and threats. Despite having reached out to a number of people at my school including the headmaster (principal) deputy head (vice principal) the response was very dismissive, as the threats were getting worse, I spoke to my headmaster again, I was no longer feeling safe, I was in tears, I asked if he had spoken to the girls, he told me he would try if he had time, he told me I was being over sensitive and that I should not let it get to me. All he did was make me feel that I was being a nuisance. I even tried reaching out to my English Teacher in a journal, but to no avail. Even my mother went into the school to meet with the deputy head, his attitude was 'girls would be girls' but would look into it! This was a month before the event!

The year was 2006 it was Friday, January 2. At recess, I was in the computer room when two girls came and told me that they wanted to make up with me. I knew a bit of their character by then and knew that she would not want to apologise in front of others, so it would have to be out of sight! The girls lead me to the washroom. As soon as the door was opened, I was ambushed. I did not stand a chance, I was leapt on by the leader who head-butted me, pulled my head down and repeatedly kicked me in the head. Then she grabbed the sides of my head and swung my head full force into the brick wall. I collapsed onto the floor. A dinner lady had apparently heard all the noise outside and came in! We were all made to go outside. Despite having been found on the floor, no medical help was sought.

After lunch I went to my lessons. I now know that the feelings I was experiencing were that I was going in and out of consciousness. I was too scared to tell anyone. I was confused and frightened. I was also afraid that no one would help, and it would become worse because of the previous experience of having asked for help before! My vision was blurred at times and my hearing was off. I felt nauseous, and some of my senses felt numb.

I was picked up that day by a friend of the family, she had apparently relayed to my mother, her concerns with how pale I was looking and how quiet I was on the journey home! I eventually told mom, what had happened! I was seen at the hospital but unfortunately, it was not picked up at that time that I had in fact sustained a subdural hematoma. I am lucky to be alive! We were told that there was probably some swelling and bruising, and I was sent home. Nobody fully understood the severity of the attack at that time, it was months later that it became more apparent just how bad it was.

Mom and dad, went with me to the school on Monday to meet with the headmaster. He acknowledged that he had heard about the attack, but yet did nothing to see if I was ok. Due to the ferocity of the attack, the school had been informed that the police would be involved. The headmaster was not happy about this.

The main leader was given a two-day exclusion. When I returned to school, she boasted of having been taken on a shopping trip by her mother on one of the days. She was eventually arrested and charged with unprovoked attack, which basically meant that as a minor, very little other than remaining on her record until eighteen and it would then be wiped clean provided she did not assault anyone else.

When I eventually returned to school, despite dealing with ongoing headaches, I was now dealing with taunting and threats from the girls. To make matters worse, one of the teachers was also a bully, he would make comments like 'doing a Jade' when someone had taken time off dealing with a headache. He did not just make fun of just me, but others too. He would often make sarcastic comments, especially towards those who were slower in the class. He seemed to like getting the laughs at the expense of others.

Things were just getting worse. Late one evening the girls had called our home threatening to hurt me again. I couldn't take it anymore, they had worn me down, I was terrified, I collapsed to the floor in tears, I just wanted to die. I did not return to the school after the phone call as despite my parents having notified the school, their attitude was that it had happened outside of school hours. Looking back it was easier for the school to have just let me go as they very much relied on an influx of funding from a huge local company.

The school's general attitude on bullying was, "Not at our school." In later years a very kind counsellor stepped forward on my behalf and that of others saying that there was indeed a huge issue with bullying at the school by both students and teachers. He admitted there was a lack of discipline and following of procedures on behalf of the school administration. I am happy to now report that very shortly after I left the school and due to other reasons that I am legally unable to state, both the headmaster, deputy head and some of the teachers have since been replaced. New anti-bullying policies have been put in place and should be available to all students, parents and guardians. I continue to hope and pray that they are followed and acted upon!

Sadly, my story does not end there, that year we moved to Canada. I am now a proud citizen, but neither I or my poor family had any idea of just how much worse things would get.

Towards the end of 2006, my headaches started to increase in both quantity and severity. I saw a general practitioner here and was referred to the Children's Hospital under Brain Injury. It was there that doctors confirmed that I had depleted blood particles from a subdural hematoma that would coincide with the timeline of the assault. I started on a medication and underwent rehabilitation and help from a counsellor at the hospital. Sadly, over time the migraines started to take a toll on my mental well-being. I started to become depressed, anxious and was also dealing with what I now know to be PTSD! On one of the many visits to the ER my symptoms were so severe that upon examination it was thought that I may have had a tumour as a papilledema was believed to be seen. I had to endure a lumbar puncture, it was difficult for the doctor to get it into the site area, the pain was excruciating.

In addition to dealing with this pain I was also experiencing what they said was a gall bladder spasm as a result of the morphine that had been administered for the head pain and pressure. The doctor had to go into the site area at the base of my spine a total of three times before being able to draw fluid to check the pressures. I was then sent for an emergency scan, not sure if it was a CT or MRI. My mom throughout remained calm, supportive and strong, but I could see it in her eyes, she too was scared. I was hospitalised with post lumbar puncture trauma and what was eventually diagnosed as Persistent Post Concussion Syndrome. It was a worrying time as I was constantly vomiting, losing vision, hearing, having numbness down one side of the body and often in excruciating pain. At least I did not have a tumour that was the one saving grace out of this.

After discharge from the hospital, I continued to get the migraines, some worse than others. My ability to deal with them got worse and so did my depression, and the recurring night terrors, which I now know to be PTSD. My ability to focus in junior high lessened and my relationship with both, what I believed to be the love of my life and my first real boyfriend and my friends started to deteriorate.

I started to self-harm, I hated myself, I felt guilty for hurting people around me even though I now know I did not mean to. I was hurting, I did not want to live anymore dealing with the pain and awful nightmares. It would be easier for me to not be alive anymore. I started to go down a very dark road, I was first hospitalized under mental health for suicidal ideation. This was just the first of a few occasions, of being sectioned for my own safety, the longest spell in hospital was for a three-month period. On one occasion my mom came down to my bedroom to apparently find me on the floor in my own vomit. Little did she know that I had been drinking and using street drugs. In fact, I had intentionally tried to overdose multiple times, but had vomited so much and my mom found me in time, that probably saved my life multiple times!

I attended my grade 9 graduation. Very shortly after is when I was admitted to hospital for a three-month period. I look at my photos from back then, my smiles were hiding so much pain. I think I looked happy on the outside, but was going on inside was very dark. Following discharge from hospital I then went into a day treatment program, I did very well and graduate. Everyone was hopeful, including myself, I would do well for a while. I attempted to attend high school to do grade 10 but the migraines, anxiety and PTSD continued to get worse. One day when I was apparently found hiding under the stairs at school, my parents were called. My attendance once again became sporadic. I started to self medicate with street and prescription drugs as none of the medications seemed to be working. I was referred to two different alternative schooling programmes in which I got introduced to stronger drugs by other students who were also troubled! Please do not get me wrong, these alternative options are great for many, but at that time I was hell bent on self-destruction and escaping from my pain and PTSD. I would seek out anything, where and when I could, I didn't care anymore, not even for my amazing Mother and family.

My ongoing behaviour, which was sometimes volatile, led to my Mom calling Social Services begging for their help. Yes, ironic, my Mother, the best possible Mother you could want or need asking for Social Services to intervene, because I was not the one being hurt. At first, they did not want to be involved. They even went to my siblings' school, and again did not feel it necessary to be involved. Mom was persistent and explained that she was concerned for her other children's safety and she was insistent on them helping as it was due to unusual circumstances. They finally agreed, but said my mom was too good at what she did as a parent so they helped to advocate for my safety out of the home. They supported my parents when I went missing and my mom had to attend court to get various orders for my safety. This would often take hours at a time, but not as many hours as my mother and father spent scouring the streets of downtown Calgary at night and during the day looking for me.

I no longer wanted to feel pain, or to remember. I got deeper and deeper into alcohol use and street drugs. The next part of my story is ugly and I apologize, but it is important for people to have a better understanding of how life's circumstances can lead them into such depravity, this is a time in my life I am not proud of.

I have to do a lot of work on myself to try and forgive myself. I purposely lived on the streets and in shelters for a number of weeks, months. This time is a blur apart from some incidents, that will remain with me for life. I chose to live like this despite having a loving home and caring parents, purely so I could self medicate because at that time conventional medications were not working. I have since found out that this is a common practice amongst either victims of crime, abuse or other.

On one occasion I lost all self-respect after I woke up somewhere downtown Calgary, missing parts of my clothing and bleeding. I found out from a number of other street kids that I had been raped whilst passed out on alcohol and drugs. I was disgusted with myself, I felt dirty and worthless. Shortly after I miscarried. This drove me into a deeper depression and a self-destructive pattern. I sought and stole alcohol and drugs. I was hooked, did not care whether I lived or died, at the time I would have preferred the latter. On at least one occasion after being coerced by what I now know to be a pimp and being hooked on drugs and alcohol, I was used to procure money. I did not care at that time what happened to me, I just did not want to feel the pain and to be quite honest did not care if I even lived.

It is now believed that with my mum's determination and investigation work a Protection of Sexually Exploited Children order was able to get me off the streets, my memory is not great, so not sure if this came before or after the order. The support they offered was a reputable live in support system. They took me in as it was not deemed safe for my siblings at that time for me to be living at home. Sadly, this turned out to not be the case.

Again for legal issues I cannot go into too much detail, but can say that this agency and its staff are now closely monitored. One of the caregivers was heavily using Oxycontin and was extremely dependent on it. I was able to access with ease oxycontin, at that time my drug of choice to help numb everything and it worked...temporarily. Even under their care, I had attempted to overdose, this was covered up by the individuals. Upon finding out that I was able to obtain drugs in the residency, my Mother apparently contacted Social Services and told them what was happening and that I needed moving to a safe house as I had become at risk. It was based outside of Calgary, a two-hour drive my family would visit regularly. They never gave up on me. I have no idea if my story is in chronological order up to this point, but at least I do know that my mom, dad and brothers and sister love me. Their story and the impact of what has happened to me and how it has affected their lives may never be heard!

All along on my journey, my rock, my mother, my angel without wings has been there for me and so has my amazing father, who, although not by blood, has been my dad since I was 4. At times my mom has had no choice but to use tactics that I know are against her gentle nature. She even had to stand up against my psychiatrist at one time when he was not going to admit me. She knew, I do not know how but she knew that I was planning on ending it. She had always respected him and it was very difficult for her, to go against his judgement, but she was right to do so. If it had not been for her, I would not be alive and here to tell some of my story!

On another note, I would also like to thank Demi Lovato. Yes, she is famous, but she has no idea what impact she had on my life and how she helped inspire me to live and to get through some of those very difficult times. Mom wanted to arrange a meet and greet but could not afford it, but at least she and dad were able to get tickets for me and my beautiful little sister to see her in concert, I am blessed.

This is not my entire story, but hopefully enough of it to make people understand where the effects of bullying can lead. Sadly, in some circumstances things can be even worse, there is loss of life. I consider myself one of the lucky ones. Even as I write my story, I am dealing with vomiting while trying to write, due to dealing with another migraine that has now been going on all day.

What is there to gain from my story? Nothing, other than the hope that you listen and talk to your children, that you reach out for help, whether an adult or a child, know that you are not alone and that there are more resources now than there were when I was younger. If you need help, get it! Never give up on your child!

I want to end my story on a positive note, despite knowing that I will have to deal with my struggles with debilitating pain, back and head pain due to headaches, Basilar migraines or cluster migraines; loss of peripheral field vision on my left side, vasovagal syncope (passing out due to chronic pain) chronic anxiety disorder, borderline personality disorder (due to head injury) and be on Assured Income for the Severely Handicapped (AISH) for the rest of my life, I still consider myself to be one of the lucky ones. I get to tell my story - many don't!

I remain forever hopeful that things will improve not only for me, but for society as a whole. Bullying is real. It exists, in schools, homes, workplaces, and more. For kids and adults, we all have a responsibility to help stop it. My mom, despite having three other children, two of which are on the Autism Spectrum; one with a rare bone deformity, resulting in painful surgeries, has started Families Impacted by Bullying (FIBB). She has some amazing friends who are supporting, helping and encouraging her with her volunteer work. It took her a while to finally pluck up the strength and courage to start it, due to her own life experiences, some of which are regarded bullying, but that is a whole other story. It is her story. It is also difficult for her, juggling this and the needs of her other children, but she is determined to try and make a difference.

I want to give hope to others. I am now 21. Although I am on medications for chronic pain and my mental health issues, I am determined to remain hopeful for the future. I feel so blessed to have a loving and patient family, an amazing partner who has been so supportive and patient with me with my ongoing struggles. He and I are expecting what we hope to be a healthy baby. Although not planned, I am very pregnant. Even though the pregnancy was not planned, I can guarantee that this baby will be very much loved and cherished. My partner and I are looking forward to the little one's arrival. In fact, he can feel the baby moving already, which gives us so much happiness. After all I have been through, I finally know there is a future and a bright one. My hope is that by the time our little one is ready to start school that better laws are put in place and reinforced; that the prevention methods, education and supports will help alleviate, if not eradicate bullying.

In time as I continue to hopefully grow even stronger emotionally. I hope to be able to tell some of my story at presentations. I also want to help reach out to other young people who are dealing with a variety of issues, by using my own life experiences. I dream of being able to work one day, maybe as a youth counsellor or in the mental health profession, how realistic this is, I do not yet know, but I continue to hold onto hope for a healthier and happier future.

GINA DICKASON

I am the founder of Families Impacted by Bullying Founder/Director, and Jade's mother.

FIBB is a grassroots charity, still awaiting registration, but whilst doing so is still doing the work to try and help prevent another child from being hurt or worse, or another family from struggling both emotionally and financially due to supporting their bullied child or worse a grieving family due to the loss of their child as a result of bullying!

We are currently running a Zip It campaign, which involves handing out bracelets and leaflets explaining the meaning behind them, which is twofold. "If you do not have anything nice to say, say nothing or Zip It on the flip side. If you see bullying taking place, do not be a bystander, go and tell an adult, you could just save someone's life". As we are only a small charity we have to very much rely on fundraising. We have a wonderful photographer who has partnered with us and who feels very passionate about what we are trying to accomplish, she has helped launch the 'Be Your Own Hero' campaign. We feel that we need to teach our children at a younger age how to stand up for themselves, to have a voice and to show character, despite what is occurring around them. We feel that with compassion, friendly and positive support, we can help children understand how they can be an influence for good, against bullying. We know we can't eradicate it, but we wish we could just ZAP it for good!

We are about PREVENTION, AWARENESS, EDUCATION and SUPPORT regarding Bullying & the issues surrounding it!

PREVENTION! Through our fundraising efforts, we hope to get 'Buddy Benches' into as many schools as possible, we are currently working on a more community based initiative and are excited about working on getting this the first of our preventative measures in place! Running presentations! In time we want to offer a number of different workshops, some of these will be done with the collaboration of other agencies!

AWARENESS! We will be running a number of campaigns throughout the year, bringing about awareness of how we can bring about change!

EDUCATION! We wish to be able to distribute and run information presentations and workshops on how to deal with situations of Bullying, whether it be in schools, workplace, home or other. This will also involve letting people know their rights as far as the law goes & the consequences when breaking the law surrounding bullying issues!

SUPPORT! At this point we are only able to offer advice and give moral support, due to lack of funding, however, it is hoped that we will eventually be able to offer free counselling services to both victims & their families! Workshops, to include, but not restricted to Art Therapy, Relaxation Therapy, Self Esteem & Self Image, and one day! Having first hand experience of the huge financial strain it can have on a family dealing with issues surrounding bullying, support with financial struggles when going through a crisis!

Our biggest goal would be to have a FIBB Centre in every

province/state! Where people are able to access various resources and help, whether they are the victims or the ones who are doing the victimizing.

It has to be remembered that although it does not make things right and in any way excuse the behaviour of Bullies, there is more often than not a reason why they do what they do to others. Many themselves are also being victimised. We need to reach out to them too, and help them to turn their behaviour around. Before their actions lead them into causing physical or psychological damage to others or worse, causing someone's child to take their life.

If anyone would like to reach out and help us achieve our goals, they can do so by emailing us at familiesimpactedbybullying@gmail.com. All donations are greatly appreciated, no matter how small.

***

Visit **Be Your Own Hero** at www.christinaparkerphotography.com/be-your-own-hero

Find Families Impacted by Bullying on Facebook.

CRAZY PETE

My father was a popular man in Arborg, even though his ideas were different from most people's and his attitudes were uncompromising. On Saturday afternoons he and I would park the straight job in the garage with the rest of the trucks and then drive the family '63 Pontiac over to the Legion. It was a short drive around the block, down the gravel street and then down the two blocks of paved main drag to where my mother worked. The Legion was new in 1965 and it was designed to be reminiscent of an airplane hangar, so it only had windows on the north and south ends of the building. The entrance was around the east side of the building. We swung into the parking lot and went in through the enclosed main door. A half dozen steps through the vestibule and you were into the main space. The first thing that always hit me when we went in was the smell of air-conditioning. It was the smell of luxury to one of six kids from a family getting by on the salary of a truck driver and a barmaid.

My mother was usually behind the serving bar, leaning on the counter to be part of any conversation that was happening on the floor. My father would whisper a quick little "Hello" to my mother before he sat down. She did not want him to be too familiar with her even at the best of times.

113

Then we were in the main area which had a two storey cathedral ceiling and was divided into three equal areas, one for the Army, one for the Navy and one for the Air Force, each marked out with its own distinctive flag mounted on the high west wall. It was a wonderful place with a full sized pool table at one end in the Navy part of the floor; a big shuffleboard table along the wall with a lit-up score display mounted above the middle of the board, looking like the display of a pinball game. We always sat at a table in the central Army section of the Legion, my dad with his double rye and Pepsi and me with my Mountain Dew and bag of chips.

The table we sat at was always different depending who was already sequestered there before us. There would be the welcoming hails and then, depending on the amount of time that had passed since the last encounter, the handshake or pat on the back and always the warm smiles and round of gentle ridicule. On a hot sunny summer's afternoon in Manitoba the clientele of the Legion were dressed in grey-green work clothes, some with their sleeves rolled up, all with their caps hung on the arm of their chair. From the floor to ceiling windows of the north wall there was the amber light through the whiskey in their glasses or the sparkle of yellow dancing off the bubbles in their glasses of draft. Cigarettes were held between tough nicotine stained fingers made thick from years of hard labour in the fields. Their tanned and wind burnt faces topped with hair slicked down by the caps that shielded their eyes from the sun and the rain. These things made them everything a man and my father's friends should be.

But often I would be reminded that my father was different from these men. It was something that the conversation would eventually expose. It was a flaw deep within them and it would occasionally surface, like a Goldeye that had grown brave nibbling at the paler fish under the surface of the lake and had come up in the hope of more interesting prey. It was a distance that kept my father apart from these men no matter how much they might have in common.

"I hear you got Crazy Pete working with you at the Transfer. Isn't that more trouble than it's worth? You've got'a tell him how to do every fuckin' thing. Oops, pardon me Mary," one man said. He owned a farm and had hired Pete Sororchuk to help him out once or twice before.

My father took the cigarette out of his mouth, smiled, sipped at his whiskey, and looked with his bright grey eyes at the farmer. My father was a real hard working man, not just some kind of soft handed chauffeur, his body straight and hard. He could break loose a 14 foot corrugated steel culvert from the back of his truck and toss it out into the ditch as though it were a fence post.

"Hasn't Pete worked for most of you? Didn't you get a full day out of him?"my father asked.

"Yeah and then he's off to the pub pissing it up till he shits his pants!" Tony fired back.

"Listen Tony, if those other guys back at the garage worked as hard as Pete, maybe I wouldn't have to go looking for help every time I have to unload my truck. And maybe he wouldn't get so drunk if people didn't encourage him," my father said.

"Maybe, but I don't like having him around and the wife doesn't like him around neither."

"But that's just the point," my father said. His face focused, the light from the sun off of the bright white cenotaph in the courtyard outside reflected in his eyes. "If you didn't drive him back to town where he's only gon'na go to the pub. If you had him for supper and he spent more regular time with people, then he'd probably know how to behave."

"Mary, you'd better cut off your husband's drinks. He's had enough," the farmer said. "Or maybe not, maybe we all need another round. This kind of talk makes me think of church meetings and we all need a stiff shot to get over those."

Everyone laughed, including my father, who held his cigarette in his teeth up at an angle and smiled good naturedly. But I knew that he wasn't laughing inside, that he would finish his drink and on the last sip wink at me and then wave goodbye to everyone and he, my mother, and I would leave their Saturday-afternoon good humour intact.

On the way home, he didn't talk, but instead pretended that he was interested in my mother's talk about the gossip she had heard from the ladies in the Legion. The sun was bright off the river as we drove home along it. The willows along the bank were an intense yellow green and the grass on the banks stretched out rich emerald to meet the side of the gently winding road. The North Star Creamery was already shut down for the day and as we drove past Gerry's Auto Body I could see only a few guys cleaning up before they closed.

My mother had exhausted her preamble and now was ready to talk to my father. Which usually meant that the argument would start.

"Eddy, why do you have to have a drink with that bunch? You always start an argument with them," she said.

I could see my father's eyes flick sideways at her, in the rearview mirror.

"That wasn't an argument, that was just a little disagreement," he said.

"It didn't sound like it was just a disagreement. It sounded to me like you were picking a fight with them."

"It's just that . . . those guys are a good bunch most of the time, but sometimes they don't see things right, that's all."

My mother looked at me in the back seat, her eyes smiling so he could see them. She was never one to go to war without enlisting her allies.

"Did you know that your father was an expert on how retarded people should be treated?"

"It's not a joke, Mary. Pete is poor and slow and those guys take advantage of him."

"Well you certainly haven't underpaid him," she said. " And you've lent him money any time he's asked!"

And she went on. I wished that she would just be quiet. I knew that he was feeling the same pain now that he had felt in the Legion, and my mother was compounding it with a load of guilt about how he neglected her and his children. Nobody seemed to understand him – not my mother, not the men he drank with. And, at fifteen, how could I express to him that I felt his pain?

The air suddenly became cool, the sky turned a yellowish green and it started to rain. As we pulled into the driveway, my sister stood out at the side door waiting for us. We got out of the car and she immediately bombarded my father's complaints. "Crazy Pete came looking for you while you were picking up Mom and he didn't want to leave and he's waiting inside and he's drunk."

"I don't want him drunk in my house," my mother said. "I've got supper to make."

Pete was sitting in a chair at our kitchen table when we walked in. He was a little man in dusty work clothes, but to my mother, he might as well have been a pile of manure on her clean floor. Pete smiled widely and raised his hands in welcome.

"Hi Eddy. I have been waiting here for you 'cause I couldn't find you at the garage and I need a ride home. Hi, Mary, you got a real good girl, she made me a real good cup of coffee," he said, a little too quickly and a little slurred. You could smell the beer on his breath from across the room.

"It's supper time, Pete," my father said. "And besides I'd just have to go and get you in the morning because I need some help with a load of salt for the new water treatment plant."

"So now I have to feed him, and make a place for him to sleep in my house, with him smelling like a barn!" my mother said, as she shot my father a withering glance.

I myself did not want "Crazy Pete" sleeping overnight at our house any more than my mother did. I had seen him staggering around uptown with a fresh urine stain in the front of his pants, being laughed at or avoided by anyone who happened upon him. All of the kids knew that he was a retard.

"But Dad," I piped up. "You said that Al and I could help you at the water treatment plant."

I knew damned well that Pete could outwork me, but I didn't want to lose out on the $1.25 an hour I got paid as a driver's helper. My feelings hurt a bit as well because my father was choosing the retard over me.

"I was at Oscar's pig farm all day and I'm pretty tired but if you want me to work early tomorrow, then I'll work," Pete added to the mix.

"Vernie, I told you that you could help tomorrow but that was before Bert let me know that there wouldn't be anyone from the town available to help unload," my father chided me.

Pete could see that things were tense and he wanted to help so he said, "Eddy you got lots of help, so maybe you don't need me."

The rest of the family was filing into the kitchen as was our habit when my father came home. He was usually on the road before we were awake and quite often not home 'til after supper. So when he was home we would vie for his attention. The youngest, my father's namesake, wanted to tell

Dad about his latest accomplishments and was making his way to him. My mother was reaching for something in the cupboard and bumped a plate on the counter toward the edge. Pete, eager to please jumped up to catch the dish that was in no real danger of falling. When he got to his feet, he was a little unsteady because he was a good six-pack into a drunk. He put one of his work booted feet down on top of Edward's five year old foot. I could almost hear the crunch. Edward howled and Pete jumped back as quickly as he could, but the damage was done. The tears boiled up from Edward's eyes and he got his wind into a real good wail of distress.

My father scooped him up into his arms and tried to soothe him while he looked at his wounded limb.

"It's okay, Edward. It's all right, see it's just a little scrape. There won't even be a bruise. See," he said as he wiggled Edward's foot up in the air, in an effort to cheer his little boy.

My mother surveyed the incident from her post by the stove with her hands on her hips. Pete was babbling an apology to my father and she fixed him with a glance of total disgust. Then she turned her glare toward my father.

"Eddy, you get him out of my house right now!" She barked.

My father stood there silent for a moment as he tried to think of the right thing to say to calm my mother down, knowing full well that she was going to have none of it. Then with her head shaking from the strain of her bottled anger my mother yelled, "Eddddyyy!"

We all knew that this was the precursor to an all out battle which you would be able to hear all the way down the block. And which we often did.

My father knew now that he had no choice in the matter. He set Edward down and in his own bruised anger he took Pete's arm and led him toward the door.

"Just keep my supper warm!" Then they were gone.

My mother knew that when my father left the house in a storm of wounded pride that he might not be home again 'til after the Legion or the pub was closed. She also knew that when he came home drunk the battle would resume, but it would be on his terms, and that meant that she would bear the brunt of all of his rage and frustration without any of his usual sober judgment.

"You go with your father and you make sure that he doesn't stop anywhere for a drink!"

I was down the stairs and outside before I realized that I hadn't even called my friend Alvin to see what was happening that night. Of course, there was no turning back now. And I opened the door of the car and hopped into the back seat.

"Mom said you should take me with you," I shot out to explain why I had jumped into the car as my father had just put it in gear. Then I sat back and said nothing, waiting for him to either accept my presence or tell me to get out of the car. Before my father could say anything, if he was going to, Pete commented on how quickly the storm had swept up. My father let off the brake and we backed out of the driveway.

Pete lived about eight miles out of town in the direction of Lake Winnipeg. Rather than cut back through town to take him home, my father turned east down River Road. Unlike Highway 68 the River Road was a gravel road that paralleled every twist and turn of the river most of the way out to Pete's. We drove along the road with a cloud of dust trailing off behind us like the contrail of a jet cutting across the blue prairie sky. The sun shower had not dropped enough water on the ground to keep the dust down on the country roads. But the golden light of the sun that was now low in the evening sky turned the landscape into a technicolor panorama.

Everything seemed charged with bright colour, especially against the blue violet of the retreating rain clouds and the onset of night as it pushed in from the east. No one had spoken a word since we left our house, and the silence was unrelieved as we turned off the River Road. We rolled over the Graveyard bridge and then turned again onto the highway where the whisper of the tires on the pavement replaced the low roar of the gravel road. Then, almost because the silence was too obvious, Pete had to say something.

"I didn't mean to step on Edward, I was only trying to catch that dish before it got broken," he said while he stared at his feet. Then he looked up at my father.

"It's okay, Pete," my father said, without looking away from the highway.

"I sure didn't mean to start no trouble between you and Mary!" Pete blurted.

"Don't worry about it Pete, Mary and I have problems that have nothing to do with you."

My father offered a cigarette to help Pete relax and reassure him that he wasn't angry at him. I could see Pete visibly relax. Although both of my parents smoked I wasn't interested and so the prospect of the two of the men smoking in the car was cause to open the window. I had chosen to sit on the passenger side of the back seat because if I were behind Pete then he couldn't see me and would be less likely to try and engage me in conversation. Talking to Pete always made me feel uneasy. I felt that his world was so different from mine that there was really nothing for us to talk about. I felt that superior to him.

It wasn't long before we turned off the highway and on to the gravel road that led to where Pete lived with his Aunt and Uncle. Ever since my father had told Pete that things were all right between them he had been babbling happily away. I had zoned out the conversation and was staring down at the side of the road and letting the gravel and grass blur my vision as it swept by my window. Here and there the narrow ditch was clogged with the dried husks of last year's cattails. I looked back to see the rocket trail of dust billowing out behind the car as we cruised along, listening to the buzzing call of the red-winged blackbird broken by the occasional bell tones of a rock ringing off of the exhaust pipes. Then we slowed and turned onto a narrow dirt road with the ditch a lot closer to the car. The water had that rusty red tint that spoke of iron rich soil, but I could see clear to the bottom of it. The song of the spring peepers was fading out, being replaced by the summer chirrup of the leopard frogs. Their tiny voices came to me from just beyond the rush of the tires on the carpet of the hard packed dirt road.

I sat back in my seat and saw a row of spruce trees up ahead at the end of a black furrowed field that was flushed with the bright green of new growing grain. Just behind the evergreens was a little box of a one and a half storey house. It was yellow with white trim and it seemed to glow in the golden light of the late day sun. A little way behind it were some run-down out buildings and past them a faded red barn that seemed to shine with a false glamour in the sun's light. There was a tractor and some equipment parked near one of the largest out buildings, but I saw no other immediate signs of life. We slowed as we approached the gravel driveway where the water in the stainless steel culvert reflected the sun back at us in a blinding flash of light.

The house was hidden from view behind the curtain of mature spruces until we drove through their shadow and came to rest in the driveway. A shaggy barnyard dog came barking out to the car, scattering a few chickens into a flurry of white feathers. My father and Pete got out of the car but I hung back, not anxious to find out how friendly the dog might be. An older man came round the corner of the house and began talking to my father and Pete. The dog came sniffing around the car and stopped by the window, its tail wagging eagerly. I had been bitten a couple of times, and, being full of the fear that I carry to this very day, I was slow to trust animals. However, this dog was obviously not going to bite me. I got out of the car and walked over to my father's side with the mutt skipping enthusiastically around me.

My father stopped talking to the old man and turned to Pete. He told Pete that he should show me his place. I had no idea why my father would think that I would be even slightly interested in Pete's room. Pete was pleased with this plan and seemed as excited as the dog was with my presence. This only made me more reluctant to follow Pete, especially since I saw that my father was not joining us.

"Vernie, you go with Pete, see what he's got."

He said it in a warm but insistent way that reassured me and aroused my curiosity at the same time. So I followed Pete. He led me away from the house toward one of the outbuildings, so I suspected that he was going to show me some wild animal that they had captured or some newborn puppies.

We walked up to an eight by twelve foot shack of grey unpainted wood with ancient red shingles upon its weather-beaten roof. The tongue and groove siding took on a sharper focus in the bright gold light of the setting sun. Each of the hairs on the nape of Pete's neck cast its singular shadow on the weathered skin it sprung from. Pete was talking in a melodic voice warning me of his excitement over what he was about to show me. This made me even more wary of what he had in store for me.

Pete stepped into the unlit building; a slash of sunlight cut through the interior of the hovel. The light illuminated the small embarrassed pallet of a bed with its rumpled bedclothes and ticking mattress. The bed had been made from raw 2 by 4's and built into the 2 by 4 structure of the shanty. There was a small box of a cupboard on the wall closed with a striped cloth curtain that hung from a string stretched between two nails tapped into either of the top corners of the frame. The floor was unfinished tongue and groove planking. Across the meagre floor from the bed was a small square table which sat under the only window in the tiny cell. There was a box and some junk on the mean surface. Then I realized why the stuff had caught my eye. It wasn't junk - it was a couple of the tab trays that model parts came attached to. Pete opened up the box and took out a nearly complete model of a World War II F-51 Mustang fighter plane. He had assembled a lot of the plane, it was ready for painting. I took it from his hands and examined it.

I began to tell him of the pitfalls of model building. I lectured him of the dangers of using too much glue and of how he must make sure the pieces fit easily together before he applied any glue at all. I felt that my father had wanted me to explain to Pete how to build a model because it was well known that I was one of the best model builders in Arborg. Other children brought models to me to assemble and paint for them. My uncle had given me his "special" 1/16th scale model of a Corvette Stingray to construct because he was afraid he might ruin it.

Pete interjected a "Yeah" and an "Uh huh" at every opportunity. I felt that he wasn't listening and thought that he was going to go ahead and wreck the Mustang because he really didn't care to learn the right way to make a model. He seemed in too much of a hurry to say something, just waiting to interrupt, not listening at all. I was frustrated with this childish adult. This man with the mind of a child.

Pete was excited to show me something and when I finally relented in my lecture he pulled back the cloth of his makeshift cupboard to reveal the treasures he had hidden there. The golden light of the sun coming through the open door now shone on models of a Hawker Hurricane, a Messerschmitt, a Spitfire and a Stuka. The models were free of any dust and their paint jobs glinted in the sun. I could clearly see the blue and red bull's eyes on the wings of the Hurricane and the Spitfire, the black and white crosses on the bodies of the Stuka and the Messerschmitt. The camouflage on them perfectly echoed the pictures of the box tops that had been cut out and propped up behind each of the models.

Pete told me about how the RCAF's No. 1 Squadron had flown Hurricanes in the Battle of Britain and how they had destroyed more enemy planes than all the other defences combined. He then went on to the Messerschmitt and how it was a great fighter plane.

"Faster than the Hurricane! Almost as fast as the Spitfire! The Spitfire had a maximum speed of 355 to 454 miles per hour depending on the mark. The Spitfire was produced in 22 marks."

A cold hard part of me reassured myself that he was reciting what he had memorized off the model box. It was the part of me that was surprised to find that Pete knew more about something than I did. I had noticed that Pete had no airbrush or cans of spray paint in his little summer house. He had painted the fuselages of his little planes with a brush, using the tiny bottles of Testor's model paint that sat in a row in his cupboard. The edges of the brown and green camouflage on the Hurricane were clean and there were no brush hairs in the paint of any of the models. I knew that I couldn't have done a better job myself, but what challenged and impressed me was the camouflage on the Messerschmitt and the Stuka. The

125

camouflage on these models was not hard edged areas of colour. The yellow-green and dark-green of the Stuka were blended into each other. The paint on the originals would have been airbrushed on but Pete had reproduced the effect with his sable hair brush. This, I knew I could not have done.

At this moment I really looked at Pete. He was a small man, no more than five foot eight. The sun was shining on his unshaven face, glinting off each strand of stubble, giving it a salt and pepper appearance. His thick black framed glasses enlarged his eyes and blurred them in the glare of the evening sun. I could see the sparseness of his body through the faded plaid shirt he wore and yet I could also see the strength in his hands and the dirt under his fingernails. I saw the poorness of his clothes. Work clothes for a working man. And I was drawn back to his eyes as he spoke and as I looked into them again, I still saw nothing of the ability to paint so meticulously and assemble the plastic planes so carefully. I wondered if my father had somehow seen something there that I had not or could not.

For a moment, everything that I was, was challenged by the achievements of this little man. My brilliance in school in the sciences, my excellence in art, the arrogance and the innocence of my youth. I suddenly saw myself as a small defenceless thing exposed to the uncaring world. How many times have I been called 'a retard'? How many ways had my footsteps paralleled those of Pete Sororchuk?

Then my father's solid silhouette filled the doorway and sheltered me from the harsh light of the sun. His presence provided me with just enough relief to regain the foothold of my battered innocence. When he asked me what I thought, I was able to muster enough conceit to hesitate before I complimented Pete on his models. We passed around the models and Pete and my father and I exchanged what we knew about the planes and then we said our goodbyes and got in the car and were on our way.

In no time we were heading back to Arborg on Highway 68, facing into the blinding glare of the setting sun. My father lit a cigarette with the dash lighter and adjusted his sun visor. We had not spoken a word since we left Pete's. I could not pull myself out of the introspective mood I found myself in. I had decided that I would not tell Alvin of Pete's skills since we had been competing with each other for months as to who had the superior model building skills. I was trying to console myself with the concept that Pete was some kind of savant, and considered purchasing some airplane models and showing my Dad what I could do. I looked across the river at the outskirts of town, then looked over at my father. He sat behind the wheel, watching the road with the shadow of the visor cutting across his wind burnt face.

"Make sure you tell Alvin that I will need both of your help tomorrow and he can sleep over. It's probably a good idea." He took a drag on his cigarette and then it returned in his hand to the steering wheel.

"I heard that Pete fell on his head when he was a kid and that's why he is retarded now."

"Who told you that? Pete was born with Down's syndrome."

"Alvin heard it from his uncle."

"You know, not all retarded people look mongoloid. It depends on how severely affected they are.

"Vernie, Pete hasn't got all of the opportunities that you have. What he does have going for him, is that he isn't afraid to work and the Transfer needs men like him. So you shouldn't resent him getting work that you could handle. To you, it's a little spending money, but to Pete it's a luxury. Understand?"

"Yeah."

"Good. And I hope I don't hear you making fun of Pete with the other boys anymore."

"No. Don't worry, I won't."

And I didn't. I didn't buy any airplane models either. That was Pete's area of expertise and I wasn't going to take that away from him. Later, when I saw that Pete was headed for trouble, I would try to look out for him. Or if he was being exploited by one of the older men I would let my father know.

My father and I were to become estranged over the passing years. It was when he was diagnosed with lung cancer that I opened my heart to him again. It was then that I thought of how the best lessons are taught by example and of how even through the shortfalls in our relationship, caused by his alcoholism and my misunderstanding, my father had always tried to show me what the best of a man is. The morals that I have today are the ones he gave to me when he was at his best, and the ones he tried to keep, even at his worst.

Bullying Stops Here!

RESOURCES

A study on bullying by the University of British Columbia, based on 490 students (half female, half male) in Grades 8-10 in a B.C. city in the winter of 1999, showed:

64 percent of kids had been bullied at school.

12 percent were bullied regularly (once or more a week).

13 percent bullied other students regularly (once or more a week).

72 percent observed bullying at school at least once in a while.

40 percent tried to intervene.

64 percent considered bullying a normal part of school life.

20-50 percent said bullying can be a good thing (makes people tougher, is a good way to solve problems, etc.).

25-33 percent said bullying is sometimes OK and/or that it is OK to pick on losers.

61-80 percent said bullies are often popular and enjoy high status among their peers.

WHAT IS BULLYING?

Many children have a good idea of what bullying is because they see it every day! Bullying happens when someone hurts or scares another person on purpose and the person being bullied has a hard time defending themselves. So, everyone needs to get involved to help stop it.

Bullying is wrong! It is behaviour that makes the person being bullied feel afraid or uncomfortable. There are many ways that young people bully each other, even if they don't realize it at the time. Some of these include:

- Punching, shoving and other acts that physically hurt people.
- Spreading bad rumours about people.
- Keeping certain people out of a group.
- Teasing people in a mean way.
- Getting people to gang up on other people.

The four most common types of bullying are:

Verbal bullying - name-calling, sarcasm, teasing, spreading rumours, threatening, making negative references to one's culture, ethnicity, race, religion, gender, or sexual orientation, unwanted sexual comments.

Social Bullying - mobbing, scapegoating, excluding others from a group, humiliating others with public gestures or graffiti intended to put others down.

Physical Bullying - hitting, poking, pinching, chasing, shoving, coercing, destroying or stealing belongings, unwanted sexual touching.

Cyber Bullying - using the internet or text messaging to intimidate, put-down, spread rumours or make fun of someone.

What are the effects of bullying?

Bullying makes people upset. It can make children feel lonely, unhappy and frightened. It can make them feel unsafe and think there must be something wrong with them. Children can lose confidence and may not want to go to school anymore. It may even make them sick.

Some people think bullying is just part of growing up and a way for young people to learn to stick up for themselves. But bullying can have long-term physical and psychological consequences. Some of these include:

- Withdrawal from family and school activities, wanting to be left alone.
- Shyness
- Stomach aches
- Headaches
- Panic Attacks
- Not being able to sleep
- Sleeping too much
- Being exhausted
- Nightmares

If bullying isn't stopped, it also hurts the bystanders, as well as the person who bullies others. Bystanders are afraid they could be the next victim. Even if they feel badly for the person being bullied, they avoid getting involved in order to protect themselves or because they aren't sure what to do.

Children who learn they can get away with violence and aggression continue to do so in adulthood. They have a higher chance of getting involved in dating aggression, sexual harassment and criminal behaviour later in life.

Bullying can have an effect on learning.

Stress and anxiety caused by bullying and harassment can make it more difficult for kids to learn. It can cause difficulty in concentration and decrease their ability to focus, which affects their ability to remember things they have learned.

Bullying can lead to more serious concerns.

Bullying is painful and humiliating, and kids who are bullied feel embarrassed, battered and shamed. If the pain is not relieved, bullying can even lead to consideration of suicide or violent behaviour.

How common is bullying?

Approximately one in 10 children have bullied others and as many as 25% of children in grades four to six have been bullied. A 2004 study published in the Medical Journal of Pediatrics found that about one in seven Canadian children aged 11 to 16 are victims of bullying. Studies have found bullying to occur once every seven minutes on the playground and once every 25 minutes in the classroom.

In the majority of cases, bullying stops within 10 seconds when peers intervene, or do not support the bullying behaviour. Students are most vulnerable to bullying during transitions from elementary to junior high

133

school, and from junior to senior high school.

There is a correlation between increased supervision and decreased bullying. Bullies stop when adults are around.

WHAT CAN YOU DO?

A re you being bullied? Do you see bullying at your school? There are things you can do to keep yourself and the kids you know safe from bullying.

Treat Everyone with Respect

Nobody should be mean to others. Stop and think before you say or do something that could hurt someone. If you feel like being mean to someone, find something else to do. Play a game, watch TV, or talk to a friend.

Talk to an adult you trust. They can help you find ways to be nicer to others. Keep in mind that everyone is different. Not better or worse. Just different. If you think you have bullied someone in the past, apologize. Everyone feels better.

What to Do If You're Bullied

There are things you can do if you are being bullied. Look at the kid bullying you and tell him or her to stop in a calm, clear voice. You can also try to laugh it off. This works best if joking is easy for you. It could catch the kid bullying you off guard.

If speaking up seems too hard or not safe, walk away and stay away. Don't fight back. Find an adult to stop the bullying on the spot.

There are things you can do to stay safe in the future, too. Talk to an adult you trust. Don't keep your feelings inside. Telling someone can help you feel less alone. They can help you make a plan to stop the bullying.

Stay away from places where bullying happens. Stay near adults and other kids. Most bullying happens when adults aren't around.

Protect Yourself from Cyberbullying

Bullying does not always happen in person. Cyberbullying is a type of bullying that happens online or through text messages or emails. There are things you can do to protect yourself.

Always think about what you post. You never know what someone will forward. Being kind to others online will help to keep you safe. Do not share anything that could hurt or embarrass anyone.

Keep your password a secret from other kids. Even kids that seem like friends could give your password away or use it in ways you don't want. Let your parents have your passwords.

Think about who sees what you post online. Complete strangers? Friends? Friends of friends? Privacy settings let you control who sees what. Keep your parents in the loop. Tell them what you're doing online and who you're doing it with. Let them friend or follow you. Listen to what they have to say about what is and isn't okay to do. They care about you and want you to be safe.

Talk to an adult you trust about any messages you get or things you see online that make you sad or scared. If it is cyberbullying, report it.

Stand Up for Others

When you see bullying, there are safe things you can do to make it stop.

Talk to a parent, teacher, or another adult you trust. Adults need to know when bad things happen so they can help.

Be kind to the kid being bullied. Show them that you care by trying to include them. Sit with them at lunch or on the bus, talk to them at school, or invite them to do something. Just hanging out with them will help them know they aren't alone.

Not saying anything could make it worse for everyone. The kid who is bullying will think it is ok to keep treating others that way.

Get Involved

You can be a leader in preventing bullying in your community.

Find out more about where and when bullying happens at your school. Think about what could help. Then, share your ideas. There is a good chance that adults don't know all of what happens. Your friends can go with you to talk to a teacher, counsellor, coach, or parent and can add what they think.

Talk to the principal about getting involved at school. Schools sometimes give students a voice in programs to stop bullying. Be on a school safety committee. Create posters for your school about bullying. Be a role model for younger kids.

Write a blog, letter to the editor of your local newspaper, or tweet about bullying.

Cyberbullying Statistics

90% of parents are familiar with cyberbullying; 73% are either very or somewhat concerned about it.

2 in 5 parents report their child has been involved in a cyberbullying incident; 1 in 4 educators have been cyber-harassment victims.

73% of educators are familiar with the issue and 76% believe cyberbullying is a very or somewhat serious problem at their school.

Educators consider cyberbullying (76%) as big an issue as smoking (75%) and drugs (75%).

The study adds that "the most commonly experienced form of cyberbullying is when someone takes a private email, IM, or text message and forwards it to someone else or posts the communication publicly"

38% of girls online report being bullied, compared with 26% of online boys.

Nearly 4 in 10 social network users (39%) have been cyberbullied, compared with 22% of online teens who do not use social media.

BULLYING ON SOCIAL MEDIA

You are supposed to be aged 13 or over to have an account on a social networking site like Facebook, Twitter, Myspace or Bebo. If you ever come across anything on the internet, whether it's on a social networking website or anywhere else, where people are making suggestions to you that make you feel uncomfortable or upset, please tell your parents or another adult.

Most social networking sites prohibit bullying and other abusive behaviours which include harassment, impersonation and identity theft. If you need to make a complaint, you can copy the terms and conditions which have been breached and take a screenshot of the comment or photo as evidence.

How to report bullying or abuse on social media

Facebook - Facebook does not tolerate bullying and say they will remove bullying content when they become aware of it and may disable the account of anyone who bullies or attacks another. You can report bullying on Facebook using the report links which appear near the content itself.

Twitter - If you receive a tweet or reply that you don't like, you can unfollow that person. If they continue to contact you, you can block the user (just click on the heart icon on their profile and select block user). If you continue to receive unwanted replies and it feels abusive, you can report it.

Myspace - To report abuse such as inappropriate content, please visit the violator's profile and click on the 'Report Abuse' link underneath their main photo. A member of staff will personally review all reported violations.

YouTube - flag a video you think is inappropriate (click on the little flag bottom right of the video) and YouTube will take a look at it to see whether it breaks their terms of use. If it does, then they will remove it. YouTube rules say you can't upload videos with hate content, nudity or graphic violence and if you find one on someone else's space, click on the video to flag it as inappropriate.

Safety tips

Keep it private - Don't post anything on a social networking site which gives your real name, address, school, phone number or which will allow a stranger to contact you in real life. Make sure you don't ID your friends either.

Don't upload anything that might embarrass you at a later date. You might not realise it, but things you post on the internet now could come back to cause problems for you later on, for instance, when you go for an interview for college or a job. If you have a webcam never be pressured into taking pictures of yourself that you wouldn't want other people to see.

If you're using a shared computer at school, in an internet cafe or library, then you'll stay logged on even when you close the browser. So don't forget to log off when you've finished the session. Read more
140

about staying safe online.

Protecting your tweets - On Twitter you can choose to protect your tweets so that people can only follow you if you approve them first. You can select this by going into the 'settings menu' then 'security and privacy' and ticking the box for 'protect my tweets'.

Location settings - Many social networks like Facebook and Twitter allow you to post your location each time you tweet or post a status update. This might seem like fun for your friends to know where you are, but it can also mean that people you don't know will see where you are, especially if you're tweeting from your mobile on a profile that is public. To turn off the location settings, go into the 'Settings' menu, scroll down 'Security and privacy' then to 'Tweet location' and untick the checkbox that says 'Add a location to my tweets'. You can also press the button that says 'Delete all location data', to clear information about where you've been in the past.

Inappropriate behaviour

If anyone makes you feel uncomfortable or embarrassed online, then please tell your parents or another adult. If they're doing it to you, then they might also be doing it to other young people. It's particularly important never to meet up with anyone you meet online in real life, if anyone suggests that to you, and particularly if they suggest you keep it secret that's a real danger sign.

When you go into a social networking site people might approach you to be a friend, but remember that no matter how much they tell you about themselves, they are still strangers and they might not be telling you the truth. There have been cases of adults pretending to be young people to chat to them online and try and involve you in inappropriate activities. This is called grooming and is a criminal offence. CEOP (The Child Exploitation and Online Protection Centre) investigates cases of sex abuse and grooming on the internet. You, your parents, or anyone else who is concerned, can report incidents by clicking the red button on the top right hand corner of the CEOP website.

Although the police can get information from your computer's hard drive, it's helpful if you don't delete anything you think is dodgy until the police have decided whether they need it as evidence.

Removing or blocking friends

Facebook - click on their profile, then on the 'message' button dropdown and you will see the option to 'unfriend'. You can also block a person this way.

Twitter - to remove or block someone on Twitter, click on the button with a head icon on it next to the 'Follow' button on a user's profile. If you click on this you will see a menu with the options to BLOCK the user to prevent them from seeing your profile, and vice versa, and you can also REPORT FOR SPAM, which will alert Twitter to any users who are abusing the service.

Myspace - You can remove people from your Friend List so they can't add comments to your profile page, you can delete comments on the profile page and you can delete messages they send. You can also view their profile and click "Block User" so they can't contact you again.

YouTube - go to your account page and click on "All Contacts" link in the "Friends and Contacts" section. Choose which person you want to unfriend and the click on "Remove Contacts". From then on the person won't be on your "Share Video" list.

Closing your account

Facebook - to deactivate your Facebook account, go to the "settings" tab on the Account page. That will remove your profile and content and nobody will be able to see your details or search for you. But if you decide to reinstate the account later then the whole lot will be restored, including your friends and photos.

Myspace - click on "Account Settings" and then on "Cancel Account". The cancel confirmation page then shows and you should click the red button which says "Cancel my Account". You can give a reason or not, it's up to you. Click "Cancel my Account" again and an email will be sent to the user's email address. When the email arrives, click on the link to finish the process and confirm that you want the account removed. If the email doesn't arrive have a look in your email spam folder to see if it is there. If you're a parent and you don't receive the email, remove all the content from your child's profile and in the 'About Me" section type "Remove Profile". You can also set your profile to private so that nobody else can see it.

Twitter - on the settings tab on your profile, you will see 'deactivate my account' at the bottom. Click on this to delete your account. You have 30 days to change your mind.

YouTube - click on "My Account" in the top right hand corner and under "Account Settings" click on "Delete Account". Give the reason you're quitting the site and your password and then click "Delete My Account". Log out by clicking the link in the top right hand corner. Your videos will be removed from the site immediately and the thumbnails will disappear as soon as YouTube is updated. Your profile is removed permanently.

Avoid online fights or posting offensive material

Don't get into arguments online, this is called flaming and it can get nasty. If you break the rules of whichever site you're on then the content is likely to be removed and you might have your membership

143

terminated. You're not allowed to upload anything which is offensive or racist and which promotes physical harm so don't make threats to anyone. Neither are you allowed to harass people or to encourage other people to harass them. You're not supposed to ask for personal information from anyone under 18 either, so if you are under 18 and anyone asks you, for instance, where you go to school, make sure you report them.

Spreading rumours

Don't spread rumours or make up false things about a friend you have fallen out with. You are not allowed to upload anything which is threatening, abusive or which is defamatory. It's defamatory if you say untrue things about someone which give them a bad reputation they don't deserve. It can also be harassment, which is a criminal offence.

You're not supposed to upload a picture or video of someone without their permission either. Never set up a social networking website account in the names of other people or upload false information about them.

BULLYING AT HOME

All families will occasionally argue, but changes at home such as a parent losing their job, an illness, a new baby or a marriage breakdown can cause serious conflict. Also, a new marriage creating a stepmother or father, along with stepbrothers or sisters, moving into the home will change the dynamics of a family. An adult or sibling can have problems with drugs, alcohol or other substances which may create bullying behaviour.

Bullying in the home can be physical violence or verbal and emotional abuse. Sometimes it includes both.

Verbal abuse and emotional abuse can include name calling, constant faultfinding or nit-picking, never giving praise or not even acknowledging your existence. The bully may try to set people within the family against each other by telling lies about the other person to provoke arguments.

Bullying at home can make you feel very alone and frightened. A bully in the home is also the most difficult because it is very hard to admit that in the sanctuary that is your home, where one would normally feel safety and security, you feel afraid, anxious, and hopeless.

- your partner

- your family

- your neighbours

- your friends

Many times when one is being bullied at home it is by their partner. When you hear the word "love " you probably do not want to believe that the person you have chosen to share your home and life with could be capable of harming you. This is very dangerous because when you love someone you have a higher tolerance, allowing them to get away with more than others. It is also very hard because you feel an obligation to your partner because you made promises to each other that you may not want to break, making it nearly impossible to speak out against him or her.

When your partner is bullying you, it is also can be impossible to tell anyone because you do not wish to have people believe that your relationship is anything less than perfect, and you may also be concerned if any children are involved.

You may be wondering where you draw the line between sibling rivalry and ostracizing you from the family. The family unit is a solid foundation to anyone's life, and many adults say their family defined who they are. However, beneath this happy appearance can be a hidden menace.

A casual fight between you and your mother or father can turn into them leaving a mark on you forever. If they repeatedly pick another sibling over you, it can lead to you feeling left out. Double standards are most definitely a form of bullying. You may, however, decide to brush it under the rug as though you somehow were supposed to be learning something or deserved it and you don't. It is important to know that bullying happens repeatedly and for no apparent reason.

Sometimes if you're being bullied within the family and the person may not even realize what they are doing to you. This doesn't mean you

146

should just brush every offence under the rug if you repeatedly feel as though they are bullying you and they do not stop after you bring it to their attention, then you may wish to seek outside assistance.

Your friends are also very close to you. They may even be like family, but a friend can bully you as well. A friend can take advantage of you and make you do stupid things to be in their group. You can also have a friend that treats you as a convenience friend meaning that they are only friends with you when it makes them look good or they gain something from it, but other times they say mean and hurtful things behind your back.

The first thing you must realise is that this person is not really your friend and what he or she is doing is wrong. A real friend would not make you earn their friendship or change who you are, if you wish to remain friends with them. A friend is someone you are yourself with. If for any reason they make you harm yourself or do things that you know are wrong, then they are bullying you. They may play on your emotions to make you give them things like money or objects they say they will return, then never do. The best way to deal with this would be to remove yourself from this person or group of people.

The last place that you may encounter a bully on home is your neighbours. Because these people live in such a close proximity to you, it is very rare that you will never have any interaction with these people. A neighbour can cause you distress by deliberately playing the radio too loud at two in the morning or parking their car in front of your home so that you cannot. Though these things may seem trivial, they are a form of bullying because they are taking control of bits and pieces of your life that you are meant to be in control of. The less trivial things are if your neighbour tries to get you evicted out of your apartment because they have a personal grudge against you that you seem to know nothing about.

Bullies have many faces, including people we love the most.

There are many ways that bullies in the home environment can choose to strike, but regardless of how it is done it is terribly hurtful.

- Face-to-face
- Online
- Through others
- Through fear

By taking away

- Your sense of belonging
- Your feeling of safety
- Your value
- Your control

One of the many ways that a bully can attack you is face to face. Now this can range from verbally insulting you in front of other family members, such as children, to take authority away. If a child sees you being disrespected and bullied by your parent or partner, they will believe that they do not need to respect you either.

A bully can also start a conversation and proceed to openly mock you in front of friends to make you appear unintelligent. When a bully has the ability to make you feel worthless in front of others, then they know that they have the ability to control the conversation at hand. When you lose control of a conversation or of a situation, it makes you vulnerable meaning the bully has won.

They want you feel as though you have no control so that they can step in and control you for their own selfish gain. A face to face conflict could also turn into physical abuse. A bully uses face to face bullying because they are able to see you in fear and that is what drives them. A bully likes bullying because they want to feel better about themselves through controlling you. Another way a bully can control you is through other family members. A sibling, for example, could bully you into believing that you do not agree with them over a certain situation, then they will turn a parent or another valued family member against you. It goes back to sibling rivalry, only unlike when a child says "I didn't do it. He or she did!" it is a fierce competition for affection.

Most family units centre on a number of things, but it may come down to children. If you are being bullied by your parent or partner they could threaten to take your child or children away from you so through the threat of you losing your children, you let your parent or partner bully you. A bully could also go out and turn others against you so that they can stay far away from the situation.

If someone is trying to bully you in the family, they may turn other members against you so that at a family gathering, perhaps for the holidays, no one will talk to you or they will start saying mean things about you because of the bully that planted those ideas in their heads. If the bully is someone respected within the family unit, it can be especially difficult. This can become very distressing, because if the bully starts turning the rest of your family against you, they are taking away your security and safety net.

Your family is supposed to be the ones who take care of you and protect you from the rest of the world and seeing that as humans we are naturally sociable creatures, we need that sense of belonging to survive without that safety net a person has been left completely open to whatever the bully's wishes are. A bully knows that there is power in numbers because they are one person trying to make you feel as lonely as they do so they want to take away people they know will back you up. In this case, the bully will purposefully put you in situations where you will feel left out of what is happening and eventually you will feel out of place even in your own home environment.

If you do not feel safe or you feel as though you do not belong anywhere, they will be able to better take advantage of you. Most of all, a bully wants you to be afraid and worthless. A bully in the home environment will do this by taking away your responsibility or making you do more work than you normally would because your partner refuses to share the load. If your spouse is bullying you, they may use threats to bring fear to you such as losing your house, possessions, children or anything else that they know you value.

Bullies are very creative in the way they choose to go about hurting their targets. In the family, it is very easy for the bully because they know you very well, perhaps too well, and that is a perfected tactic that a bully uses. They want to know your greatest fears so that they can use whatever it is against you to try to destroy you. Again, the thing to remember is to know the difference between joking around and when someone is seriously attempting to hurt you and take the necessary precautions to protect yourself and the ones you love.

SIBLING BULLYING

A lot of the time, people confuse sibling bullying with sibling rivalry; they are not the same. This is a situation that can escalate quickly and get out of hand if the proper measures are not taken.

What is Sibling Bullying?

Sibling bullying is a form of violence that takes place between siblings. This kind of bullying is common when siblings are children, but it can also carry into adulthood, which is known as adult sibling bullying.

Many parents overlook the warning signs of sibling bullying. Bickering back and forth between siblings is common and expected, but there is a line that should not be crossed. There are four warning signs that parents should be on the lookout for which include:

- Foul insults
- Physical aggression
- Destruction
- Ganging up (common when more than 2 siblings are involved)

Foul Insults - Foul or harsh insults are the common warning signs of sibling bullying. Insults can do more damage to a child than physical abuse. Words can do a lot of damage to a child, especially when it comes from someone within their immediate family. Harsh insults can kill a child's self-esteem, causing them to have issues later on in life. Common insults of sibling bullying include, "you're not pretty", "you're fat", "you're the stupidest person I know", and "you will be a failure all of your life." Any form of negativity from one sibling to another should be addressed immediately.

Physical Aggression - Children can become extremely frustrated because their emotions are still new to them, and they may not know how to sit down and discuss the things that are bothering them. Instead, they lash out at their siblings, which is a form of physical aggression. This form of aggression can be categorized as:

- Biting
- Hair pulling
- Scratching
- Kicking
- Hitting

Although siblings are expected to disagree on different things and have arguments, physical aggression should not be tolerated under any circumstances.

Damage/Destruction - Many children have been known to throw things and have tantrums, but there is a line that should not be crossed. Damage to anything or pure destruction can result in one sibling destroying another sibling's favorite item, such as a toy, or an item that is similar. Sometimes pets are targeted as a way to hurt their sibling.

The **"Gang Up"** - Siblings can gang up on each other when there are three siblings or more. Two siblings may gang up on the other, causing an unfair fight. There is one sibling who is left out, and the consequences of this for the lonely sibling could one day take a turn for the worst. Depression and anxiety could develop, just to name a few.

Causes of Sibling Bullying

There are a few causes of sibling bullying that some parents are not aware of.

Unwanted - Some children feel unwanted by their parents, and this can sometimes cause sibling bullying to occur.

Frustration - All children are not privileged to live in a safe neighborhood, have food to eat, and clothes to wear. A child can become frustrated under these circumstances and take it out on their siblings.

Playing the Parent - A lot of the time, the oldest child has to "play the parent". When children are forced to play the parent, they do everything the parent is supposed to do, such as cook, clean, help younger children with their homework, bathe their younger siblings, get their siblings ready for school, and things that are similar. A child who plays the parent role does not have a chance to enjoy their childhood because they are forced to take on a responsibility that is not theirs too early in life. This much responsibility can cause a child to become depressed, have anxiety, and lose sight of their goals.

Jealousy - Jealousy is common among siblings, but this situation can take a turn for the worst. Some parents make this situation worse by showing one child more attention than the other. Sometimes this form of jealousy is made up in a child's mind, and sometimes it is not.

Another reason jealousy would become an issue between siblings is because one sibling is achieving more than the other. No one wants to be considered a failure, and when one sibling feels that the other is succeeding and achieving more goals than the other sibling, sibling bullying can become an issue.

Ways to Stop Sibling Bullying in Your home

Stop Aggressive Behaviour - Aggression should be stopped immediately. Name calling and fighting are signs of aggression that should not be tolerated. In this situation, an adult needs to intervene immediately and talk with the children.

Holding Accountability - Bullies need to know that bullying is a choice and is not a necessity. Regardless of the child's reasons for their actions, they need to be held responsible for the things they say and do.

Remove Jealousy within the Home - In this situation, the best thing to do is diffuse the jealousy within the home and have a talk with your child and find out what's bothering them.

Teaching and Learning - In some situations, the parents are great role models, but the child takes a different path, often due to other influences, such as friends and their surroundings. In any event, teach your child how to respect others, especially their siblings, and teach them what being a family and a respectful citizen is about.

Empathy - Teach your child what bullying is and show them how it feels. This is a great way to teach them to identify with the situation and how it feels to be the victim in the situation.

Problem Solving Skills - Teach your child effective techniques to help them solve problems instead of expressing how they feel with anger.

Prevention - Monitor your children and see if there is a pattern. If you can identify a pattern, break the cycle, and put something positive in its place.

Sibling bullying is a lot easier to deal with than other forms of bullying. A lot of parents take comfort in the fact that they can discipline their child when something is wrong, rather than wait for the parent of the other child to take action. Sibling bullying is a common form of bullying, but that does not make it right. Children need to keep their hands and other objects to themselves. For some children, this is a lot easier said than done.

If you find yourself in this situation, it will be in your best interest to stop everything, and find out what the issue is between your children. One of the last things you want to happen is to overlook the signs of sibling bullying, and this situation has escalated into something more, and turn into adult sibling bullying when your children are older.

The International Labour Organization declared workplace harassment and violence one of the most serious problems facing the workforce in the new millennium. At the time, 75 per cent surveyed said they were bullied at work.

The Canadian Safety Council reports that 75 per cent of victims of bullying leave their jobs and that workplace is four times more common than sexual harassment or workplace discrimination.

BULLYING IN THE WORKPLACE

Workplace bullying is when a person or group of people in a workplace, single out another person in unreasonable, embarrassing, or intimidating treatment. Usually the bully is a person in a position in authority who feels threatened by the victim, but in some cases the bully is a co-worker who is insecure or immature. Workplace bullying can be the result of a single individual acting as a bully or of a company culture that allows or even encourages this kind of negative behaviour.

Workplace bullying can take many forms:

- Shouting or swearing at an employee or otherwise verbally abusing him or her
- One employee being singled out for unjustified criticism or blame
- An employee being excluded from company activities or having his or her work or contributions purposefully ignored
- Language or actions that embarrass or humiliate an employee
- Practical jokes, especially if they occur repeatedly to the same

person

There are also some things that are usually not considered workplace bullying:

A manager who shouts at or criticizes all of his or her employees. While this is a sign of a bad manager and makes a workplace unpleasant, it is not bullying unless only one or a few individuals are being unjustifiably singled out.

A co-worker who is critical of everything, always takes credit for successes and passes blame for mistakes, and/or frequently makes hurtful comments or jokes about others. Unless these actions are directed at one individual, they represent poor social skills, but not bullying.

Negative comments or actions that are based on a person's gender, ethnicity, religion, or other legally protected status. This is considered harassment and, unlike bullying, is illegal in the United States and gives the victim legal rights to stop the behaviour.

According to the Workplace Bullying Institute, up to a third of workers may be the victims of workplace bullying. About twenty percent of workplace bullying crosses the line into harassment. The New York Times found that about sixty percent of workplace bullies are men, and they tend to bully male and female employees equally. Female bullies, however, are more likely to bully other females. This may be because there is more pressure on females trying to succeed in male-dominated workplace, and more competition between females for promotions.

Regardless of its source, workplace bullying can have serious negative effects on employees, such as:

- Stress
- Absenteeism and low productivity
- Lowered self-esteem and depression

- Anxiety

- Digestive upsets

- High blood pressure

- Insomnia

- Trouble with relationships due to stress over work

- Post traumatic stress disorder

Workplace bullying is also bad for business. Some of the ways that companies suffer due to bullying include:

- High turnover, which is expensive for companies as they invest in hiring and training new employees only to lose them shortly thereafter, possibly to a competitor

- Low productivity since employees are not motivated to do their best and are more often out sick due to stress-related illnesses

- Lost innovations since the bully is more interested in attacking his or her victim than advancing the company, and the victims become less likely to generate or share new ideas

- Difficulty hiring quality employees as word spreads that the company has a hostile work environment

Because workplace bullying can be devastating to employees and companies, some companies have instituted zero-tolerance policies toward workplace bullying. In these companies, if an employee is being bullied, he or she needs to document the bullying and present the problem to the proper person in the company, usually someone in human resources or upper management. Companies with good anti-bullying policies usually hold meetings from time to time to remind employees what workplace bullying is, how to report it, and the consequences for bullying.

In some companies, however, there is a company culture of workplace bullying. Usually, companies do not purposefully support bullying, but they may develop a problem with it either through not taking workplace bullying seriously or by developing the habit of placing blame and fault finding instead of solving problems. In these companies, employees who make a case against bullies may find that the bullying only gets worse. In this situation, employees often have to either make the best of the situation or find different employment.

Employees who are or have been victims of workplace bullying should realize that it is not their fault that they are being bullied. If they are suffering negative effects from the bullying they should seek help from a doctor or counsellor and, if the bullying is ongoing, from a career advisor who can help them plan a job or career change.

THE SERIAL BULLY

This is a bully who will move from one target to another, and whose depravity is only constrained by the realisation that they have to appear normal to fit in among civilised people. One consequence is that they rarely use physical violence on their targets, resorting instead to activities that are harder for onlookers to notice, such as emotional blackmail and underhanded tactics to get their way.

A serial bully could be anyone. They are attracted to positions of authority, but not everyone in authority is a serial bully, and not every serial bully is in a position of authority. They cannot be identified by their status, but by their actions.

A serial bully gives the impression that he (or she) must have cheated his way into his role with over-embellished or false information on his application, smooth-talking his way through the interview, because he seems to lack relevant competence for his role, substituted by an over-developed ego and sense of entitlement. Some regard this character as smooth and accomplished, and yet, to others he seems to be grossly incompetent and gets irritated when he doesn't get what he wants. His behaviour is often insensitive and unintelligent, but he appears to have no idea and is equally unaware of the effect of his behaviour on others.

To some, he appears to be fuelled by anger and aggression, but he can control the outward signs much of the time and especially in front of the people he thinks he needs to impress. He vents his anger on those who do not matter to him, or on people he is actively trying to undermine. Consequently, these people are the first to see behind his facade of charisma.

At first, he gains and maintains respect by exaggerating his achievements, favouring friends and by mimicking the behaviour of respectable people. With time, even those who regard him as smooth and accomplished respect him mainly because they are frightened of not doing, believing he could turn nasty with anyone who disagrees with him.

He does turn nasty. Feeling threatened by colleagues with competence, integrity and popularity, he picks one out and projects them onto his own inadequacy and incompetence. Using unwarranted criticism and threats, he controls them and subjugates them, without a thought for the contribution they make to the organisation, or their reputation or self confidence. Sooner or later this person - the bully's "target" - realises that they are not being "managed" but "bullied", and they start to show signs of intolerance. The bully now fears exposure of his own incompetence, and takes steps to disable the target, typically by isolating them and/or destroying their credibility and reputation among peers and decision-makers, putting them out of the picture through dismissal, forced resignation or even early retirement. Once the target has gone, within about two weeks, the bully's focus turns to someone else and the cycle starts again.

Serial Bully Traits

Perhaps the most easily recognisable serial bully traits are:

- Jekyll and Hyde nature - Dr Jekyll is "charming" and "charismatic";

Hyde is "evil";

- Exploits the trust and needs of organisations and individuals, for personal gain;

- Convincing liar - Makes up anything to fit their needs at that moment;

- Damages the health and reputations of organisations and individuals;

- Reacts to criticism with denial, retaliation, feigned victimhood;

- Blames victims;

- Apparently immune from disciplinary action;

- Moves to a new target when the present one burns out.

Symptoms of a Serial Bully at work

Most cases of workplace bullying involve a serial bully, to whom all the dysfunction can be traced. A person who is being bullied may already know, or come to realise that they have a string of predecessors who have either:

- Left unexpectedly or in suspicious circumstances;

- Have gone on long term sick leave with some sort of psychological problem, and never returned;

- Taken unexpected early or ill-health retirement,

- Have been involved in a grievance or disciplinary or legal action;

- Have had stress breakdowns;

- Been over-zealously disciplined for some trivial or non-existent reason.

Any of these things can indicate some form of dysfunction in the workplace. It is not always obvious at first as to why one colleague was fired and another suddenly went off with depression. These things are confidential to those involved and tend to be explained away with plausible

163

excuses: "Bill let down a major client and we had to let him go"; "Dorothy had some personal problems and she just couldn't hack it here anymore - poor thing". Sometimes the excuses are more damning of the target: "We discovered she had been stealing and abusing clients, so we had no choice but to dismiss her". It is not until the new target scratches the surface of these misfortunes that they realise that the truth is quite different from the rumour. Where the truth is far more appalling than the corporate line, and where one person is a common factor behind all such events, the chances are that this person could fit the profile of the Serial Bully.

The same information will be available to the employer, who should be able to notice a pattern, particularly if it is highlighted in a complaint of bullying. A serial bully is likely to be doing far more damage to their business than just occasionally destroying the health and careers of competent staff members. However, employers seem to prefer not to acknowledge it and even to try and conceal it, possibly fearing the consequences of acknowledging the actions for which the organisation would be vicariously liable.

BULLYING AND THE LAW

Bullying can be a traumatic experience, and some forms of bullying can even be considered illegal. These include:

- **Threats** - whether done face to face, online, over the phone or through text messaging.
- **Assaults** - including pushing, tripping, slapping, hitting or spitting.
- **Theft of personal items** - like a backpack, books, electronic devices
- **Harassment** - repeated tormenting online, with texts, phone calls and/or emails.
- **Sexual Exploitation** - sharing videos or photos with nudity of people under 18.
- **Hate crime** - bullying based on ethnicity, sexual orientation, religious beliefs, etc.

For all of these criminal offences, it is important to notify your local police detachment or report it to Cybertips.ca. Based on the available information, the police will decide if an investigation is warranted and whether charges may be laid.

If you are a victim of bullying

- Walk away or leave the online conversation.

- Keep track of the bullying (write it down and/or save a screenshot of the online message).

- Tell a trusted adult. If you don't trust anyone or need to speak with someone urgently, contact the confidential and toll-free

- 1-800-886-6868

- Report the bullying to school administrators.

- Report criminal offences, such as threats, assaults and sexual exploitation to the local police detachment.

- Report unwanted text messages to your telephone service provider.

- Report online bullying to the social media site and block the person responsible.

If you know someone who is being bullied

Most types of bullying go on as long as someone is watching and laughing. As a bystander, know that you have the power to stop the bullying. 60% of the time, bullying stops in less than 10 seconds when someone steps in.

- If you feel it's safe to do so, tell the bully to stop.

- Find friends/students/youth or an adult who can help stop it.

- Befriend the person being bullied and lead them away from the situation.

- Report it to a teacher or school staff.

- Fill out an anonymous letter and drop it off to a teacher or any adult you trust.

Adults

If you know or think that a child is a victim of bullying, talk to them. Let them know that they can trust you and that they shouldn't deal with bullying alone.

Help them by documenting the bullying, report unwanted text messages to their telephone service provider, or cyberbullying to social media sites. Report the bullying to school administrators; and report criminal offences, such as threats, assaults, harassment and sexual exploitation to the local police detachment.

ARE YOU BEING BULLIED?

The truth about bullying is that many people brush it off as just school drama. Sometimes, the same action might be considered a joke by some people, while others will consider it bullying. Take this assessment to see whether or not everyday actions you experience (or see) are funny pranks, or if they are actually a form of bullying.

Has anyone ever posted a comment about you online that upset you?
YES - NO

Has anyone ever repeatedly teased you or called you names?
YES - NO

Has a group of people ever excluded you by refusing to let you sit at their table during lunchtime?
YES - NO

Has anyone ever physically hurt you for no reason?
YES - NO

Have you ever been made fun of because of your appearance, gender, religion, or sexual orientation?

YES - NO

Do you feel like your friends single you out and embarrass you in front of other people?

YES - NO

Has anyone you know attempted to, or succeeded in, stealing something from you?

YES - NO

Have you ever stayed home from school because you didn't want to face the people there?

YES - NO

Do you ever try to act differently around a certain group of friends to avoid being made fun of?

YES - NO

Do you feel that certain people target you for the way you act?

YES - NO

***

If you answered "yes" to any of these questions, then you may be a victim of bullying. You may brush off these events as just jokes, but these are harmful acts of bullying. Nobody deserves to be treated like that or made to feel bad. Now is your chance to put an end to bullying by getting help and reporting it. A friend, an adult, or a teacher can be great people to talk about bullying. Let them know if someone is bothering you.

CANADIAN ONLINE RESOURCES

Bully B'Ware

www.bullybeware.com

A cooperative effort from Gesele Lajoie, Alyson McLellan and Cindi Seddon, three B.C. educators, the site offers tips and strategies, stories and materials about bullying that can be ordered. Workshops can also be arranged.

Bullying.org

www.bullying.org

Canada's original bullying website, now sponsored by the Family Channel and BBI Internet. The site uses different media – writing, drawing, music film, poetry – to educate children about bullying. A finalist for the Stockholm Challenge Awards in 2001, it has been called one of the best web sites in the world for children.

The Canadian Safe School Network

www.canadiansafeschools.com

The Canadian Safe School Network (CSSN) is a national, charitable organization dedicated to reducing youth violence and making our schools and communities safer. CSSN was founded in 1997 and grew out of the Ontario Safe School Task Force. Areas for students, teachers and parents.

Kids Help Phone

www.kidshelpphone.ca

Kids Help Phone maintains a website called "Let's Talk About Bullying." Contains a page for grown ups with links to resources about bullying.

London Family Court Clinic Bullying

www.lfcc.on.ca/bully.htm

Information for parents and teachers. Information drawn from A School-Based Anti-Violence Program (ASAP), available from the Clinic.

My Gay Straight Alliance

www.mygsa.ca

This website is an initiative of Egale Canada linking educators, students and the community to a variety of resources including classroom materials, discussion forums and more.

National Film Board

www.nfb.ca/film/bully_dance/

No More Bullies. Awareness campaign that is a joint effort by the NFB and the Canada Safety Council. Endorsed by Kids Help Phone and the Canadian Association of Chiefs of Police. NFB produced the short video called Bully Dance, available with teacher's guide.

School-Based Violence Prevention Programs

www.ucalgary.ca/resolve/violenceprevention

Resource manual that presents school-based violence prevention programs that are relevant for girls and boys, young women and young men. Reviews 79 prevention programs.

Canadian Centre for Occupational Health and Safety

www.ccohs.ca/oshanswers/psychosocial/bullying.html

Bullying in the Workplace. Good general information about workplace bullying.

The Workplace Bullying & Trauma Institute

bullyinginstitute.org

Product of four American and Canadian psychologists and health workers concerned with employee bullying. Many useful materials and references. Creators of the "Blueprint for a Hostility-Free Workplace."

Need Help Now?

Call 911

1-800-SUICIDE
(1-800-784-2433)
or
1-800-273-TALK
(1-800-273-8255)

Text Telephone:
1-800-799-4TTY
(1-800-799-4889)

Military Veterans Suicide Hotline:
1-800-273-TALK (Press 1)

Suicide Hotline in Spanish:
1-800-273-TALK (Press 2)

LGBT Youth Suicide Hotline:
1-866-4-U-TREVOR

National Suicide Prevention Lifeline (US)
1-800-273-8255

DO YOU NEED HELP?

We all have friends and family who care deeply for us, even when we don't notice, who become devastated when things such as suicide because of bullying.

Please remember, nobody can help you if you don't tell them what's going on. It's okay to tell. You have nothing to be scared of or ashamed of. Be strong, be truthful and tell someone. If that someone can't help you, find someone else. Keep telling people until you get the help you need.

Life is so precious and you deserve to live yours to the fullest.

Marianne

ABOUT THE AUTHOR

With a pen in her hand and a camera hanging around her neck, southern Manitoba, Canada native, Marianne Curtis has written several thousand freelance articles for the Dawson Trail Dispatch since 1997.

Her debut publication, a memoir called *Finding Gloria*, is a source of hope and inspiration for others as Marianne reveals raw, honest details about the mental and physical abuse she suffered as a child and teenager and how she found love, healing and peace. It reached the top of the Amazon best sellers list numerous occasions in Canada, United States and United Kingdom.

Since releasing *Finding Gloria*, Curtis has raised international awareness on the effects of child abuse, bullying, mental health issues and social injustice through writing and speaking engagements on radio, newspaper, podcasts, social media and television. For this work, she received a YWCA Woman of Distinction award nod in 2013.

Contact Information
Email: mariannecurtis.author@gmail.com
Website: mariannecurtis.wordpress.com
Blog: moondustandmadness.wordpress.com
Facebook: Marianne Curtis
Twitter: writerchick68

Emerald Publications
emeraldpublication@gmail.com

35466190R00113

Made in the USA
Charleston, SC
10 November 2014